Rocky Mountain Research Station
Invasive Species Visionary White Paper

United States Department of Agriculture / Forest Service

Rocky Mountain Research Station

General Technical Report RMRS-GTR-265

November 2011

ABSTRACT

Invasive species represent one of the single greatest threats to natural ecosystems and the services they provide. Effectively addressing the invasive species problem requires management that is based on sound research. We provide an overview of recent and ongoing invasive species research conducted by Rocky Mountain Research Station scientists in the Intermountain West in order to familiarize managers with the Station and its products. We also provide several links to continuously updated web sites and a periodic newsletter that covers Rocky Mountain Research Station's invasives species research.

Keywords: invasive species, exotic, noxious, nonnative, pathogen, rehabilitation, restoration

EXECUTIVE SUMMARY

This document contains an overview of invasive species research efforts by the Rocky Mountain Research Station (RMRS) to familiarize managers with the Station and its products.

Invasive plant, pathogen, invertebrate, and vertebrate species are among the greatest threats to forest, range, aquatic, and urban forest ecosystem health. Exotic species invasions in the United States cost an estimated $120 billion annually in lost revenues and mitigation. Expanding global trade increases both the introductions of invasive species and the costs associated with preventing introductions and managing new infestations. To address these threats, a comprehensive strategy is needed with a strong research component at its core.

Damaging impacts of exotic infestations include diminished productivity, decreased carrying capacity for livestock and wildlife, lowered recreational value, increased soil erosion, decreased water quality, and loss of native species. As native vegetation becomes displaced, further alterations in natural ecosystem processes occur, including changes in fire frequency and nutrient cycling. The impacts of invasive species can be exacerbated by human activities such as disturbance, fertilization, increasing CO_2, and climate change. Exotic weeds are greatly reducing diversity and productivity of forests and rangelands; insects and pathogens are killing trees that are essential for ecosystem functions; and aquatic algae, invertebrates, and fish invaders are disrupting native fisheries and aquatic ecosystems.

Addressing the invasive species threat requires robust scientific understandings that can be used to fuel progressive management in the four action areas of: (1) prediction and prevention; (2) early detection and rapid response; (3) control and management; and (4) restoration and rehabilitation. This document describes RMRS's invasive species research and its published works.

RMRS has the broad scientific expertise to conduct multidisciplinary research on invasive species issues with special emphasis on terrestrial and aquatic habitats throughout the Intermountain West. RMRS scientists provide ecological and biological information to help managers detect and eradicate new invaders that are still confined to limited areas. (For example, DNA tools are being developed to identify and screen for potentially invasive pathogens.) For well-established, widespread invasive species, RMRS contributes to the development and testing of landscape-scale mitigation strategies to prevent further spread into new areas and to manage invasive species to ecologically and socially acceptable levels using environmentally compatible tools and integrated control programs. (For instance, RMRS scientists are refining herbicide applications to improve the efficacy of weed control.) Additionally, RMRS, in collaboration with Montana State University's quarantine facilities and entomologists from other countries, has established a very active biological control program that includes locating, screening, and introducing biological control agents with an emphasis on agent efficacy and post-release studies. Integrated research at RMRS provides management tools to restore and rehabilitate landscapes that have been degraded by diverse invasive species. RMRS scientists are working with university collaborators to develop seed mixes of native species that are competitive with exotic weeds to improve restoration and reduce weed invasion following management activities and wildfire.

RMRS scientists are extremely active in addressing all aspects of invasive species management. However, RMRS does not have a program area assigned to invasives research, so research in this area has been an ad-hoc effort by independent scientists. This document represents the physical manifestation of RMRS scientists gathering to evaluate invasive species research needs, collate current research efforts, and develop a common vehicle for disseminating research products.

Contents

Introduction

Exotic species invasions have tremendous economic and ecological impacts around the world. In the United States, invasive species cost an estimated $120 billion annually in lost revenue and mitigation expenses. As a result, former Forest Service Chief Dale Bosworth identified exotic invasive species as one of the four primary threats to the nation's forest and rangeland ecosystems. Within the Rocky Mountain region, invasive species have had particularly profound impacts. Exotic weeds are reducing diversity and productivity of forests and rangelands; insects and pathogens are killing trees that are essential for ecosystem functions; and aquatic algae, invertebrates, and fish invaders are disrupting native fisheries and aquatic ecosystems. To address these threats, a comprehensive strategy is needed that includes a strong research component at its core. Research is particularly crucial for the effective management of invasive species because the underlying causes of invasion arise from biological processes that are currently poorly understood. As a leader in resource management that oversees the largest body of public lands in the United States, Forest Service involvement will be essential to the successful management of invasive species and Forest Service Research and Development will play a critical role. The current document is an attempt by independent invasive species researchers within the Rocky Mountain Research Station (RMRS) to jointly assess invasive species research needs, collate current efforts within the Station, and develop a working group to better disseminate invasive species research products to and solicit input from our customers.

The Forest Service developed the National Strategy and Implementation Plan for Invasive Species Management (hereafter, National Strategy) in 2004 to provide a comprehensive framework for invasive species management with a stated goal to, "Reduce, minimize, or eliminate the potential for introduction, establishment, spread, and impact of invasive species across all landscapes and ownerships." To achieve these ends, the National Strategy identifies four key program elements: (1) Prevention, (2) Early Detection and Rapid Response, (3) Control and Management, and (4) Rehabilitation and Restoration. Thus, the National Strategy establishes the necessary criteria for executing invasive species management and evaluating its success within the Forest Service, emphasizing on-the-ground management and control of invasive species as indicated by the stated Success and Accountability Measures for each of the four program areas. These accountability measures describe success in terms of preventing new introductions, reducing the number of acres infested with targeted invasive species, reducing rate of spread, and increasing the number of acres restored or rehabilitated to desired conditions. However, because the National Strategy focuses on management activities, it is not clear how Forest Service Research and Development (R&D) plays into this process and how to evaluate success of R&D in the context of these management goals. Research is critical to the successful management of invasive species, but its relationship to management must be clearly defined to properly evaluate its role in the National Strategy and invasive species management.

Research contributes to invasive species management by generating new information and ideas needed to advance both our understanding of invasion ecology and implementation of sound management, and by effectively communicating this information to those directly managing the resources. Understanding the role of Forest Service R&D in invasives management and restoration of impacted ecosystems requires understanding how R&D fits into the overall Forest Service framework. The United States Forest Service is divided into three branches: R&D, National Forest System (NFS), and State and Private Forestry (SPF). Each branch is autonomous in terms of oversight and budget, and each branch has a unique role in the management of our natural resources. R&D develops new knowledge to improve the management of our natural resources through the application of science. NFS directly oversees and manages the National Forests and National Grasslands. SPF provides information and consultation to state and private land managers with direct oversight of state and private lands, thereby acting as a liaison of information for management of lands not directly overseen by the Forest Service. For Forest Service invasives research and management to be successful, R&D must develop the critical new information and transfer this information to managers, while NFS and

SPF must implement management approaches based on these research products to improve invasive species control on the ground.

The National Strategy defines goals and objectives in terms of management outcomes that are generated by NFS and SPF. Therefore, the unique role that research plays in supporting the successful implementation of the National Strategy must be explicitly defined in order to clearly identify research products and illustrate how research products provide critical information to managers for effective implementation, i.e., establish the critical linkages among research products and the ability of NFS and SPF to successfully address the goals of the National Strategy. To achieve these ends, invasive species scientists within RMRS and representatives from the NFS and SPF convened in Albuquerque, NM, in April 2006 to accomplish four key objectives: (1) identify critical information gaps within each of the four program areas of the National Strategy that must be filled before our clients can effectively manage invasive species within this region, (2) describe the research needs to fill the identified knowledge gaps, (3) identify research products and tools that are derived from the research efforts and explain how their application by managers can improve invasive species management, and (4) describe current research within RMRS that is directed toward the recognized information gaps. This approach allowed us to identify the research needs in a management context independent of ongoing research. We then assigned current research efforts to the corresponding critical information gaps to identify the resulting research products and potential management applications of these products that would fulfill the National Strategy objectives. Through this process, we were able to distinguish between research products and management products in the context of the appropriate linkage between research and management, addressing the shortfall of the National Strategy. Input from all RMRS scientists interested in or currently conducting invasives research was incorporated through this process along with input from stakeholders.

This effort also resulted in the development of an RMRS Invasive Species Working Group (ISWG). The RMRS ISWG was developed because there is no program area in the Station specifically designed to address invasive species issues. Hence, the ISWG is a collection of scientists across all RMRS Program Areas gathered for the purpose of evaluating, consolidating, and disseminating invasive species research within the Station.

RMRS Invasive Species Program Overview

The RMRS has scientific expertise in widely ranging disciplines and conducts multidisciplinary research on priority invasive species issues with special emphasis in terrestrial and aquatic habitats of the Intermountain West (Figure 1).

RMRS invasives research covers a wide array of diverse ecological and environmental gradients from arid southwest desert to mesic northern Rockies ecosystems and from low elevations of the Great Basin and Great Plains to high-elevation Rockies ecosystems. RMRS provides the basic ecological and biological information for managers to implement eradication programs for new invaders while the invaders are still confined to limited areas. For well-established, widespread invasive species, RMRS contributes to the development and testing of large-scale mitigation strategies to prevent further spread of invasives into new areas and to suppress their populations below ecological and economic thresholds of impact using environmentally compatible tools and integrated controlled programs.

The Rocky Mountain region is host to a number of invasive species. Some invasive species of great concern in this region include cheatgrass, leafy spurge, tansy ragwort, spotted and diffuse knapweed, saltcedar, white pine blister rust, 1,000 canker disease, rainbow/brook/brown trout, golden algae, and banded elm bark beetle.

RMRS research has renowned, multidisciplinary programs on diverse aspects of invasive species that span several decades (begun up to 75 years ago) with accompanying expertise, records, specimen collections, and long-term research plots. The RMRS staff works closely with land managers and other partners from domestic to international agencies and universities to incorporate scientific findings into land management plans. Tools and applications derived from science-based RMRS research are used to manage and restore forests and rangelands degraded by invasive species. Resource managers readily use these tools and applications to reduce this threat for protecting our natural resources.

A few themes of RMRS invasive species research include: (1) assessing impacts (biological, economic, and social) of invasive species in natural ecosystems; (2) developing biological control methods for invasive plants; (3) assessing the role of disturbances and forest management practices on establishment and spread of invasive species; (4) determining basic biology, ecology, and genetics of invasive species and other affected species to facilitate predictions of future impact, management, and restoration; (5) testing treatments and methods for restoring or rehabilitating invaded ecosystems and evaluating treatment consequences to native species and ecosystem processes; (6) developing technologies for molecular identification and risk assessment models for predicting and detecting current and potential invasive species; and (7) developing user-friendly technology transfer tools (e.g., web-based tools for fire effects on invasive species) that synthesize science-based information for managing invasive species.

The prior report by Butler and colleagues (http://www.fs.fed.us/rm/pubs_other/rmrs_2009_butler_j001.pdf) provides a comprehensive list of scientists working on invasive species issues that is tabulated by RMRS Program Area and FS R&D Invasives Overarching Priority Area along with contact information for each scientist and information on his or her research focus areas. The summary therein shows there are 13.4 scientist years of effort directed toward invasives research across the Station. However, a more direct way of assessing the strengths and weaknesses of the current program is perhaps to break out RMRS publications, which are the ultimate measure of research products, by taxonomic group and National Strategy category. Table 1 presents results from a simple search of the FS Treesearch database (http://www.treesearch.fs.fed.us/) for invasive species-related publications produced by RMRS using the terms exotic and/or invasive. This search is not intended to be comprehensive. It probably underestimates actual publications, as the search terms are fairly simple. In fact, pathogen studies were not well represented from this search despite an abundance of work in this area because these search terms are not commonly used to describe pathogens. For this reason, the table also includes RMRS publications cited in the pathogen section of this document. The process of assigning publications to the various categories is also rather subjective. Despite the limitations, the results provide a representative index of real products from RMRS invasives research across the different taxonomic groups and National Strategy focus areas.

The results indicate that a good deal of work has been conducted in the Station, but that research products are not evenly distributed across the categories. Invasive plants and pathogens have received the most attention and the bulk of the research has been done in the

Table 1. Summary of the number of research publications produced by RMRS and its collaborators from 1999 to 2011 that address each of the National Strategy areas for the six identified taxonomic groups. These results are not exhaustive but provide an estimation of the distribution of research products across taxa and National Strategy Areas. This table was generated by conducting a search in the FS Treesearch database using the keywords "exotic" and "invasive" for only RMRS for the period from 1999-2011. The results were then assigned to the different categories based on taxonomic group and National Strategy Area based on title and abstract such that a paper could be counted in more than one category if it addressed more than one taxonomic group or subject area. All the specific papers tabulated here are not detailed in this document, but the following taxonomic sections give overviews of some of the key and more recent work in each area. Specific studies can be found by searching Treesearch or visiting the websites listed in Table 2.

	Prediction and prevention	Early detection and rapid response	Control and management	Restoration and rehabilitation
Plants	62	19	97	106
Pathogens	29	12	98	27
Insects	4	2	4	3
Aquatic species	2	1	3	2
Terrestrial vertebrates	2	0	2	1
Totals	99	34	204	139

area of Control and Management and Restoration and Rehabilitation. Less work has been done in Prediction and Prevention and still less in Early Detection and Rapid Response. Taxonomically, the effort is very representative of the threats as most exotic pests in the Rocky Mountain West are invasive plants, and invasive pathogens present some of the greatest per capita risks. However, certain exotic insects present grave threats and there are substantial threats to aquatic ecosystems from exotic aquatic organisms. Clearly, there is a need for more work in the areas of Prediction and Prevention and Early Detection and Rapid Response, but Station efforts are quite strong in the areas of Control and Management and Restoration and Rehabilitation. The specific chapters that follow review and discuss some of these strengths and weaknesses in more detail and the final section comments on future invasives research at RMRS.

Dissemination of research results is a high priority for research and one of the key means by which the final success of the research cycle is achieved. Technical transfer efforts are discussed throughout the document in the appropriate sections and invasive species websites are compiled here in Table 2 for easy access. These websites provide a variety of products from overviews and updates of ongoing research to conference announcements, postings of the RMRS Invasives Species Newsletters, databases, and PDFs of published results.

Table 2. Websites related to RMRS invasives species research and national websites cited in this document.

Subject/title	Internet location	Primary author
Armillaria	http://forest.moscowfsl.wsu.edu/smp/docs/docs/ART-GTR-draft_web.pdf	G. I. McDonald et al.
Exotic forest pest info. sys.	http://spfnic.fs.fed.us/exfor/	N. American Forest Comm.
Fire effects on weeds	http://www.fs.fed.us/fmi/products/Zouhar_et_al_2007.html	K. Zouhar
Gypsy moth	http://www.fs.fed.us/ne/morgantown/4557/gmoth/	USDA FS
Invasive plants	http://www.fs.fed.us/rm/wildlife/invasives/	D. E. Pearson
Leafy spurge	http://www.team.ars.usda.gov/	J. L. Butler
RMRS Invasives Expertise directory	http://www.fs.fed.us/rm/pubs_other/rmrs_2009_butler_j001.pdf	J. L. Butler et al.
RMRS Invasive Species Working Group	http://www.rmrs.nau.edu/invasive_species/	D. E. Pearson et al.
Rust diseases	http://www.rms.nau.edu/rust/	B. G. Geils
Treesearch database	http://www.treesearch.fs.fed.us/	USDA FS
White pines	http://www.fs.fed.us/rm/highelevationwhitepines/index.htm	A. W. Schoettle

RMRS Invasive Species Program
Taxonomic Group Focus Areas

I. PLANTS

By Dean Pearson, Steve Sutherland, Jack Butler, Jane Smith, and Carolyn Sieg

Exotic plants dramatically impact natural communities and disrupt ecosystem services (Mack and others 2000). Although the bulk of current impacts are caused by relatively few exotic species, many additional exotics that are currently established at low levels are increasing in density and distribution and present substantial imminent threats. Additionally, new exotic plants will likely continue to be deliberately and accidentally introduced, which represents a potential pool of new invasive species. Managers have responded to the threat of invasive species in wildlands with a significant increase in the use of current management tools. However, many of the tools now being applied to wildland exotic plant management, such as herbicides and classical biocontrol, originated in intensive agricultural systems and are proving to be more challenging to apply over large areas in complex ecosystems (Pearson and Ortega 2009). Finally, exotic plant invasions are commonly exacerbated by disturbances such as wildfires, timber harvest, road building, burning, and grazing by livestock and native herbivores. The combined effects of multiple and interacting disturbances on populations of exotic plant species, especially in the face of projected climate change, are uncertain but potentially severe (Sieg and others 2010). Our National Grasslands are particularly threatened by invasive plants. Large areas of native grasslands are juxtaposed to intensive agricultural systems that serve as an almost continuous source of new invasive plants. Further, plant species widely sown as forage for livestock or roadside stabilization are invading native grasslands and adversely impacting wildlife habitat and overall biodiversity. Thus, extensive research is needed in all aspects of exotic plant invasions in the Intermountain West.

(1) Prevention. Given the continuing introduction of new invasive plants and expansion of current species, it is important to identify which new species present significant threats and which communities are most susceptible to invader impacts. This requires assessing both the causes of invasion, such as the attributes that determine invader establishment and success, and the conditions that determine community susceptibility. RMRS scientists are conducting research to identify attributes of successful plant invaders (Sieg and others 2003; Sutherland 2004; Pearson and others in press; Ortega and others in press), evaluating biotic and abiotic factors that affect invasion into native communities by notorious invaders such as cheatgrass *(Bromus tectorum)* (Chambers and others 2007; Gundale and others 2008) and spotted knapweed *(Centaurea stoebe*; Ortega and Pearson 2005; Ortega and others in press; Pearson and others ongoing). One study is systematically sampling invaders across grasslands over a 40,000 km^2 areas in the native range of Turkey and the invaded range of Montana to examine the causes of invasion for over 20 species and quantitatively rank all invaders in the native range according to distribution and impact (Pearson and others ongoing). Station scientists and collaborators are also examining how disturbances such as wildfires (Smith and others 2009b; Dodge and others 2008; Kuenzi and others 2008; Zouhar and others 2008; Fornwalt and others 2010) and management activities such as timber harvest (Wienk and others 2004; Sabo and others 2009; Wacker and Butler ongoing), salvage logging (Fornwalt ongoing), fuels treatments (Zouhar and others 2008; Owen and others 2009; Fornwalt ongoing), prescribed fire, and roads (Fowler and others 2008, Birdsall and others 2011) affect exotic plant invasions. Work is also underway to evaluate how community response to disturbance (resiliency) relates to community invasibility (Pearson and others ongoing). Recent studies are also revealing how biotic resistance from higher trophic levels may help prevent invasions (Pearson and others 2011 and ongoing). An important area for future research is developing strategies for locating and monitoring intact systems in order to target them for protection from invasion.

(2) Early Detection and Rapid Response. To reduce the spread and impact of invaders, it is necessary to understand how invaders disperse, determine where they are likely to establish and spread, develop monitoring protocols to detect new invasions, and create tools to rapidly control new populations. A priority in this regard is identifying non-invaded or little-invaded areas that can be protected from invasions. Thereafter, early detection provides the only real opportunity to locally eradicate new populations of invasives; however, because these new populations tend to grow exponentially, the window of opportunity is brief. RMRS staff are developing bioclimatic models to prioritize areas for preventing the spread of invaders (Warwell ongoing) and strategies for monitoring exotic species presence in Forest Inventory plots (Rudis and others 2006), on Forest Soil Disturbance monitoring plots (Page-Dumroese and others 2009a and 2009b), and on rangelands (Anderson and others 2004). Station scientists are examining the role of roads, trails, and canyons as dispersal corridors for new invaders (Butler ongoing; Fowler ongoing); assessing the role of native species in dispersing spotted knapweed seeds (Sutherland ongoing); and developing management tools, including herbicide application protocols for eradication of cheatgrass (Sutherland ongoing) and sickleweed (*Falcaria vulgaris*; Butler ongoing) and community-based action programs to control yellow starthistle (*Centaurea solstitialis*; Pendleton and Pendleton ongoing; Meyer ongoing). Although important research is currently underway on Early Detection and Rapid Response, we need more work in this area. In particular, there is a need for research that establishes the economical value of preventing invasions from expanding compared to managing and mitigating them once widely established. Currently, not enough research and management effort is put into addressing new invasions before native populations and communities are impacted. There is also a need for more spatial modeling research to prioritize areas for protection and additional work to develop methods for monitoring and eradicating new invasions. Finally, there is a need to develop remote sensing techniques such as aerial surveys to advance detection strategies.

(3) Control and Management. Once strong invaders become widespread, few tools can effectively suppress them over large regions. Moreover, because the ecosystems are so complex, the tools can sometimes result in unintended consequences such as when non-target species are affected or the target weed is replaced by another weed (Pearson and Ortega 2009). Thus, research is required to identify the circumstances where management intervention is appropriate, improve the effectiveness of current management tools, develop new tools, and refine the applications of weed management tools to maximize their effectiveness and minimize their side effects. RMRS scientists and collaborators help managers apply ecological concepts to the management of grass invasions (D'Antonio and others 2009) and are conducting experiments to better understand resistance to and persistence of invasions (McGlone and others in press). Station scientists are examining how plant community composition changes in response to invasion by saltcedar (*Tamarix* spp.; Johnson and others 2009), and leafy spurge (*Euphorbia esula*; Butler and Cogan 2004) and spotted knapweed (Ortega and Pearson 2005), as well as studying effects of invaders on system processes (Nosshi and others 2007; Butler ongoing; Chew ongoing) and animals (Ortega and others 2006; Pearson 2009, 2010; Finch ongoing) to determine required mitigation. Scientists are working to advance weed biocontrol by advocating for comprehensive support of biocontrol that includes more complete and formal evaluations of introduction outcomes (Maron and others 2010). They are working on biocontrol of cheatgrass using native fungal pathogens (Meyer and others 2008a, 2008b; Beckstead and others 2010; Pendleton ongoing), developing new biological control agents for other terrestrial and aquatic plants (Magana ongoing; Markin ongoing), evaluating the efficacy and safety of biological control agents for leafy spurge (Butler and others 2006; Wacker and Butler 2006), spotted knapweed (Pearson and others 2000; Pearson and Callaway 2003, 2005, 2006, 2008; Ortega and others 2004, 2006; Sturdevant and others 2006; Pearson and Fletcher 2008; Ortega and others in press; Pearson and others ongoing), and yellow starthistle (*Centaurea solstitialis*) (Birdsall and Markin 2010). They are also evaluating the efficacy of herbicides (Butler 1994; Crone and others 2009; Ortega and Pearson 2010, 2011) and cattle grazing for weed control (Medina ongoing), and conducting economic assessments to prioritize areas and resources for managing invasions (Jones ongoing). RMRS scientists are conducting numerous studies to determine the effects of management activities, including fire, Burned Area

Recovery treatments, fuels treatments, and timber harvest (Zouhar and others 2008; Butler ongoing; Landres ongoing; Pendleton and Pendleton ongoing; Smith and others ongoing) on invasions.

(4) Rehabilitation and Restoration. The primary challenge in rehabilitating or restoring a site lies in identifying and reestablishing altered structural and functional components of the impacted community. Little is known about how the severity of ecosystem alterations impacts long-term sustainability, especially with regards to climate change. Even less is known regarding the restoration (requiring extensive management inputs)–rehabilitation (requiring intensive inputs) thresholds, or how they may change with time. Research is required to prioritize systems for restoration or rehabilitation, identify the residual effects of invaders following successful suppression, quantify the extent to which natural successional processes may restore systems, develop guidelines and approaches for reintroducing and reestablishing native species, and prevent re-infestation of the original invader(s) and secondary invasions. RMRS scientists are conducting research to quantify the effectiveness of various control measures at restoring native plant and animal communities and natural processes (Finch and others 2006; Smith and others 2006a, b, 2009a; Bateman and others 2008, 2009; Butler and Wacker 2010; Ortega and Pearson 2010, 2011; Finch and others in review; Chung ongoing; Collins-Merritt ongoing; Ortega and others ongoing) and to understand and prevent reinvasion and secondary invasion following weed control (Ortega and Pearson 2010, 2011; Pearson and others ongoing; Shaw ongoing). RMRS scientists are developing native seed mixes for seeding following exotic plant control and other management activities (Callaway and others ongoing), assessing the effectiveness of seeding in curtailing exotic species invasions following wildfires (Fornwalt 2009; Stella and others 2010; Peppin and others 2010), developing sources for native seed mixes (Butler ongoing; Shaw ongoing), and developing native seed propagation protocols (Meyer ongoing). Work is also being done to identify and propagate weed resistant genotypes of native species for use in restoration (Sutherland and others ongoing). Molecular markers are being used to determine historical population structure of plant species and inform target conditions for restoration (McArthur ongoing). Scientists are exploring how soil microorganisms affect shrub establishment in the presence of cheatgrass (Pendleton and others 2007), as well as the effect of herbicides used to treat cheatgrass on shrubs and associated mycorrhizae (Owens and others 2011). Research is also underway to understand human perspective on exotic plant management and restoration work (Raish ongoing). RMRS scientists have made a good start in the area of restoration research, but much more work is needed in developing restoration techniques, such as reseeding, and in understanding the factors inhibiting restoration, such as soil transformations and secondary invasions (Pearson and Ortega 2009; Pearson and others ongoing).

RMRS scientists have developed several important websites (see also Table 2) to help communicate research results to customers related to these overall products (RMRS Invasive Species Working Group http://www.rmrs.nau.edu/invasive_species//), the ecology of biological invasions and their management (Pearson and Ortega, http://www.fs.fed.us/rm/wildlife/invasives/), and leafy spurge management (Butler, http://www.team.ars.usda.gov/). RMRS is also providing information on interactions between fire and exotic plants through literature reviews of more than 100 invasive plant species in the Fire Effects Information System (http://www fs fed.us/database/feis/plants/weed/weedpage html) and is informing managers on a national scale through a "Rainbow Series" literature review on fire and exotic plants (http://www fs fed.us/fmi/products/Zouhar_et_al_2007.html, and Zouhar and others 2008). Quantitative analysis of knowledge gaps, such as that regarding fire and exotic plants (http://www fs fed.us/fmi/products/Zouhar_et_al_2007_pdfs/Chap12.pdf), can provide guidance for future research in the Intermountain West and nationally.

Literature Cited

Anderson, G.L.; Kirby, D.; Kline, D.; Butler, J.; Kazmer, D. 2004. Rapid field assessment of rangelands using COAST digital imaging system. In: Proceedings of the 19th Biennial Workshop on Color Photography Videography and Airborne Imaging for Resource

Assessment. October 6-8, 2003; Logan, UT; American Society for Photogrammetry and Remote Sensing.

Bateman, Heather L.; Chung-MacCoubrey, Alice; Finch, Deborah M.; Snell, Howard L.; Hawksworth, David L. 2008. Impacts of non-native plant removal on vertebrates along the Middle Rio Grande (New Mexico). Ecological Restoration 26(3):193-195.

Bateman, Heather L.; Chung-MacCoubrey, Alice; Snell, Howard L.; Finch, Deborah M. 2009. Abundance and species richness of snakes along the Middle Rio Grande riparian forest in New Mexico. Herpetological Conservation and Biology 4:1-8.

Beckstead, J.; Meyer, S.E.; Connolly, B.M.; Huck, M.B.; Street, L.E. 2010. Cheatgrass facilitates spillover of a seed bank pathogen onto native grass species. Journal of Ecology 98:168-177.

Butler, J.L.; Cogan, D.R. 2004. Leafy spurge effects on patterns of plant species richness. Journal of Range Management 57:305-311.

Birdsall, J.L.; Markin, G.P. 2010. Biological control of yellow starthistle (*Centaurea solstitialis*) in the Salmon River canyon of Idaho. Invasive Plant Science and Management 3:462-469.

Birdsall, J.L.; McCaughey, W.; Runyon, J.B. 2011. Roads impact the distribution of noxious weeds more than restoration treatments in a lodgepole pine forest in Montana, U.S.A. Restoration Ecology doi: 10.1111/j.1526-100X.2011.00781.x.

Bricker, M.; Pearson, D.E.; Maron, J.L. 2010. Small mammal seed predation reduces forb recruitment and abundance in semi-arid grasslands. Ecology 91:85-92.

Butler, J.L.; Parker, M.A.; Murphy, John T. 2006. Efficacy of flea beetle control of leafy spurge in Montana and South Dakota. Rangeland Ecology and Management 59:454-461.

Butler, J.L.; Wacker, S.D. 2010. Lack of native vegetation recovery following biological control of leafy spurge. Rangeland Ecology and Management 63:553-563.

Chambers, J.C.; Roundy, B.A.; Blank, R.R.; Meyer, S.E.; Whittaker, A. 2007. What makes Great Basin sagebrush ecosystems invasible by *Bromus tectorum*? Ecological Monographs 77:117-145.

Crone, E.E.; Marler, M.; Pearson, D.E. 2009. Non-target effects of broadleaf herbicide on a native perennial forb: A demographic framework for assessing and minimizing impacts. Journal of Applied Ecology 46:673-682.

D'Antonio, C.M.; Chambers, J.C.; Loh, R.; Tunison, J.T. 2009. Applying ecological concepts to the management of widespread grass invasions. In: Inderjit, R.L., ed. Management of Invasive Weeds. Netherlands, Springer: 123-149.

Dodge, R.S.; Fulé, P.Z.; Sieg, C.H. 2008. Dalmatian toadflax (*Linaria dalmatica*) response to wildfire in a southwestern USA forest. Ecoscience 15:213-222.

Finch, Deborah M.; Galloway, June; Hawksworth, David. 2006. Monitoring bird populations in relation to fuel loads and fuel treatments in riparian woodlands with tamarisk and Russian olive understories. In: Aguirre-Bravo, C.; Pellicane, Patrick J.; Burns, Denver P.; Draggan, Sidney, eds. 2006. Monitoring Science and Technology Symposium: Unifying Knowledge for Sustainability in the Western Hemisphere. Proc. RMRS-P-42CD. Fort Collins, CO: U.S. Department of Agriculture, Forest Service, Rocky Mountain Research Station: 113-120.

Fornwalt, P.J. 2009. Lessons from the Hayman Fire: Forest understory responses to the scarify-and-seed postfire rehabilitation treatment. Fire Management Today 69(3):39-43.

Fornwalt, P.J.; Kaufmann, M.R.; Stohlgren, T.J. 2010. Impacts of mixed severity wildfire on exotic plants in the Colorado Front Range. Biological Invasions 12:2683-2695.

Fowler, J.F.; Sieg, C.H.; Dickson, B.; Saab, V. 2008. Exotic plant species diversity: Influence of roads and prescribed fire in Arizona ponderosa pine forests. Rangeland Ecology and Management 61:284-293.

Gundale, M.J.; Sutherland, S.; DeLuca, T.H. 2008. Fire, native species, and soil resource interactions influence the spatio-temporal invasion pattern of *Bromus tectorum*. Ecography 31:201-210.

Hansen, A.K.; Ortega, Y.K.; Six, D.L. 2009. Comparison of ground beetle (Coleoptera: Carabidae) assemblages in Rocky Mountain savannas invaded and un-invaded by an exotic forb, spotted knapweed. Northwest Science 83(4):348-360.

Johnson, T.D.; Kolb, T.E.; Median, A.L. 2009. Do riparian plant community characteristics differ between *Tamarix* (L.) invaded and non-invaded sites on the Upper Verde River, Arizona? Biological Invasions. doi: 10.1007/s10530-009-9658-2.

Kuenzi, A.M.; Fulé, P.Z.; Sieg, C.H. 2008. Effects of fire severity and pre-fire stand treatment on plant community recovery after a large wildfire. Forest Ecology and Management 255:855-865.

Mack, R.N.; Simberloff, D.; Lonsdale, W.M.; Evans, H.; Clout, M.; Bazzaz, F.A. 2000. Biotic invasions: Causes, epidemiology, global consequences, and control. Ecological Applications 10:689-710.

McGlone, C.M.; Sieg, C.H.; Kolb, T.E. 2011. Invasion resistance and persistence: Established plants win, even with disturbance and high propagule pressure. Biological Invasions 13:291-304.

Meyer, S.E.; Beckstead, J.; Allen, P.S.; Smith, D.C. 2008. A seed bank pathogen causes seedborne disease: *Pyrenophora semeniperda* on undispersed grass seeds in western North America. Canadian Journal of Plant Pathology 30:525-533.

Meyer, S.E.; Nelson, D.L.; Clement, S.; Beckstead, J. 2008. Cheatgrass (*Bromus tectorum*) biocontrol using indigenous fungal pathogens. In: Kitchen, S.G.; Pendleton, R.L.; Monoco, T.A.; Vernon, J., comps. Proceedings—Shrublands Under Fire: Disturbance and Recovery in a Changing World. June 6-8; Cedar City, UT. Proc. RMRS-P-52. Fort Collins, CO: U.S. Department of Agriculture, Forest Service, Rocky Mountain Research Station: 61-67.

Nosshi, M.I.; Butler, J.L.; Trlica, M.J. 2007. Soil nitrogen mineralization not affected by grass species traits. Soil Biology and Biochemistry 39:1031-1039.

Ortega, Y.K.; McKelvey, K.S.; Six, D.L. 2006. Invasion of an exotic forb impacts reproductive success and site fidelity of a migratory songbird. Oecologia 149:340-351.

Ortega, Y.K.; Pearson, D.E. 2005. Strong versus weak invaders of natural plant communities: Assessing invasibility and impact. Ecological Applications 15:651-661.

Ortega, Y.K.; Pearson, D.E. 2010. Effects of picloram application on community dominants vary with initial levels of spotted knapweed (*Centaurea stoebe*) invasion. Invasive Plant Science and Management 3:70-80.

Ortega, Y.K.; Pearson, D.E. 2011. Long-term effects of weed control with picloram along a gradient of spotted knapweed invasion. Rangeland Ecology and Management 64:67-77.

Ortega, Y.K.; Pearson, D.E.; McKelvey, K.S. 2004. Effects of biological control agents and exotic plant invasion on deer mouse populations. Ecological Applications 14:241-253.

Ortega, Y.K.; Pearson, D.E.; Waller, L.P.; Sturdevant, J.J.; Maron, J.M. In press. Population-level compensation impedes biological control of an invasive forb and indirect release of a native grass. Ecology.

Owen, S.M.; Sieg, C.H.; Gehring, C.A. 2011. Rehabilitating Downy Brome (*Bromus tectorum*)-invaded shrublands using imazapic and seeding with native shrubs. Invasive Plant Science and Management 4:223-233.

Owen, S.M.; Sieg, C.H.; Gehring, C.A.; Bowker, M.A. 2009. Above- and belowground responses to tree thinning depend on the treatment of tree debris. Forest Ecology and Management 259:71-80.

Page-Dumroese, D.S.; Abbott, A.M.; Rice, T.M. 2009a. Forest soil disturbance monitoring protocol Vol. I Rapid Assessment. Gen. Tech. Rep. WO-82a. Washington, DC: U.S. Department of Agriculture, Forest Service. 31 p.

Page-Dumroese, D.S.; Abbott, A.M.; Rice, T.M. 2009b. Forest soil disturbance monitoring Protocol Vol. I Rapid Assessment. Gen. Tech. Rep. WO-82b. Washington, DC: U.S. Department of Agriculture, Forest Service. 64 p.

Pearson, D.E. 2009. Invasive plant architecture alters trophic interactions by changing predator abundance and behavior. Oecologia 159:549-558.

Pearson, D.E. 2010. Trait- and density-mediated indirect interactions initiated by an exotic invasive plant acting as an autogenic ecosystem engineer. American Naturalist 176:394-403.

Pearson, D.E.; Callaway, R.M. 2003. Indirect effects of host-specific biological control agents. Trends in Ecology and Evolution 18(9):456-461.

Pearson, D.E.; Callaway, R.M. 2005. Indirect nontarget effects of host-specific biological control agents: Implications for biological control. Biological Control 35:288-298.

Pearson, D.E.; Callaway, R.M. 2006. Biological control agents elevate hantavirus by subsidizing mice. Ecology Letters 9:443-450.

Pearson, D.E.; Callaway, R.M. 2008. Weed biocontrol insects reduce native plant recruitment through second-order apparent competition. Ecological Applications 18:1489-1500.

Pearson, D.E.; Callaway, R.M.; Maron, J.L. 2011. Biotic resistance via granivory: Establishment by invasive, naturalized and native asters reflects generalist preference. Ecology 92:1748-1757.

Pearson, D.E.; Fletcher, R.J., Jr. 2008. Mitigating exotic impacts: Restoring native deer mouse populations elevated by an exotic food subsidy. Ecological Applications 18(2):321-334.

Pearson, D.E.; McKelvey, K.S.; Ruggiero, L.F. 2000. Non-target effects of an introduced biological control agent on deer mouse ecology. Oecologia 122(1):121-128.

Pearson, D.E.; Ortega, Y.K. 2009. Managing invasive plants in natural areas: Moving beyond weed control. In: R.V. Kingley, ed. Weeds: Management, Economic Impacts and Biology. New York, Nova Publishers: 1-21.

Pearson, D.E.; Ortega, Y.K.; Sears, S. In press. Darwin's naturalization hypothesis up-close: intermountain grassland invaders differ morphologically and phenologically from native community dominants. Biological Invasions.

Pendleton, R.L.; Pendleton, B.K.; Warren, S.D.; Johansen, J.R.; St. Clair, L.L. 2007. Shrub establishment in the presence of cheatgrass: The effect of soil microorganisms. In: Sosebbe, R.E.; Wester, D.B.; Britton, C.M.; McArthur, E.D.; Kitchen, S.G., comps. Proceedings: Shrubland Dynamics—Fire and Water. August 10-12, 2004; Lubbock, TX. Proc. RMRS-P-47. Fort Collins, CO: U.S. Department of Agriculture, Forest Service, Rocky Mountain Research Station: 136-141.

Peppin, D.; Fulé, P.Z.; Sieg, C.H.; Beyers, J.; Hunter, M.E. 2010. Post-wildfire seeding in forests of the western United States: An evidence-based review. Forest Ecology and Management 260:573-586.

Rudis, V.A.; Gray, A.; McWilliams, W.; O'Brien, R.; Olson, C.; Oswalt, S.; Schulz B. 2006. Regional monitoring of nonnative plant invasions with the forest inventory and analysis program. In: Proceedings of the Sixth Annual Forest Inventory and Analysis Symposium. September 21-24, 2004; Denver, CO. Gen. Tech. Rep. WO-70. Washington, DC: Department of Agriculture, Forest Service: 49-64.

Sabo, K.E.; Hart, S.C.; Bailey, J.D. 2009. The role of disturbance severity and canopy closure on standing crop of understory plant species in ponderosa pine stands in northern Arizona, USA. Forest Ecology and Management 257:1656-1662.

Sieg, C.H.; Denslow, J.S.; Huebner, C.D.; Miller, J.H. 2010. The role of the Forest Service in nonnative invasive plant research. In: Dix, M.E.; Britton, K., eds. A dynamic invasive species research vision: Opportunities and priorities 2009-29. Gen. Tech. Rep. WO-GTR-70. Washington, DC: U.S. Department of Agriculture, Forest Service: 35-41.

Sieg, C.H.; Phillips, B.; Moser, L. 2003. Exotic and noxious plants. In: Frederici, P., ed. Restoration Handbook for Southwestern Ponderosa Pine Forests. Washington, DC: Island Press: 251-267.

Smith, D. Max; Finch, Deborah M.; Hawksworth, David L. 2009a. Black-chinned hummingbird nest-site selection and nest survival in response to fuel reduction in a southwestern riparian forest. The Condor 111(4):641-652.

Smith, D. Max; Finch, Deborah M.; Gunning, Christian; Jemison, Roy; Kelly, Jeffrey F. 2009b. Post-wildfire recovery of riparian vegetation during a period of water scarcity in the southwestern USA. Fire Ecology Special Issue 5(1):38-55.

Smith, D. Max; Kelly, Jeffrey F.; Finch, Deborah M. 2006a. Influences of disturbance and vegetation on abundance of native and exotic detritivores in a southwestern riparian forest. Environmental Entomology 35(6):1525-1531.

Smith, D. Max; Kelly, Jeff F.; Finch, Deborah M. 2006b. Wildfire, exotic vegetation, and breeding bird habitat in the Rio Grande Bosque. In: Aguirre-Bravo, C.; Pellicane, Patrick J.; Burns, Denver P.; Draggan, Sidney, eds. 2006. Monitoring Science and Technology Symposium: Unifying Knowledge for Sustainability in the Western Hemisphere. Proc. RMRS-P-42CD. Fort Collins, CO: U.S. Department of Agriculture, Forest Service, Rocky Mountain Research Station: 230-237.

Stella, K.A.; Sieg, C.H.; Fulé, P.Z. 2010. Minimal effectiveness of native and non-native seeding following three high-severity wildfires. International Journal of Wildland Fire 19:746-758.

Sturdevant, N.; Kegley, S.; Ortega, Y.; Pearson, D. 2006. Evaluation of establishment of *Cyphocleonus achates* and its potential impact on spotted knapweed. Gen. Tech. Rep. U.S. Department of Agriculture, Forest Service, Forest Health Protection, Region 1, 06-08:1-9.

Wacker, S.D.; Butler, J.L. 2006. Potential impact of two *Aphthona* spp. on a native, nontarget *Euphorbia* species. Rangeland Ecology and Management 59:468-474.

Wienk, C.L.; Sieg, C.H.; McPherson, G.R. 2004. Evaluating the role of cutting treatments, fire, and soil seed banks in an experimental framework in ponderosa pine forests of the Black Hills, South Dakota. Forest Ecology and Management 192:373-393.

Zouhar, K.; Smith, J.K.; Sutherland, S.; Brooks, M.L. 2008. Wildland fire in ecosystems: Fire and nonnative invasive plants. Gen. Tech. Rep. RMRS-GTR-42-vol. 6. Ogden, UT: U.S. Department of Agriculture, Forest Service, Rocky Mountain Research Station. 355 p.

II. Pathogens

By Ned B. Klopfenstein and Brian W. Geils

Invasive fungal pathogens have caused immeasurably large ecological and economic damage to forests. It is well known that invasive fungal pathogens can cause devastating forest diseases (e.g., white pine blister rust, chestnut blight, Dutch elm disease, dogwood anthracnose, butternut canker, Scleroderris canker of pines, sudden oak death, pine pitch canker) (Maloy 1997; Anagnostakis 1987; Brasier and Buck 2001; Daughtrey and others 1996; Furnier and others 1999; Hamelin and others 1998; Davidson and others 2003; Gordon and others 2001). Furthermore, invasive pathogenic fungi have disrupted many forest ecosystems and threaten to eliminate some tree species (Liebhold and others 1995). RMRS research has historically emphasized white pine blister rust, caused by *Cronartium ribicola*, because of the extensive damage to five-needled white pines that are a keystone species to many forest ecosystems in the Interior West since its introduction to North America in the late 1800s. However, this disease continues to spread to new areas and environments. RMRS scientists are instrumental in providing synthesized information concerning research on invasive species, including white pine blister rust (Geils and others 2010; Hunt and others 2010; Kim and others 2010c; Richardson and others 2010a; Zambino 2010). Another emerging invasive pathogen in the Rocky Mountain region and elsewhere is *Geosmithia morbida*, the cause of 1,000 cankers disease. This disease can cause mortality of walnut trees (*Juglans* spp.) and is transmitted by the walnut twig beetle, *Pityophthorus juglandis* (Tisserat and others 2009). In recent years, RMRS has not had the resources to address this disease. Currently, a research group from Colorado State University is evaluating methods to prevent movement of the pathogen and insect vector.

In 2006, the USDA Forest Service R&D Invasive Species Strategic Program Area obtained input from a formal peer review of diverse user groups in order to develop long-term planning for the program. The Invasive Species Strategy was revised to reflect this guidance, and research efforts were prioritized to address the future challenges to managers. As a result of this process, a publication series was produced (Dix and Britton 2010) that includes 12 visionary papers developed to address future invasive species research issues and priorities. RMRS scientists who work on invasive pathogens contributed to papers on overarching priorities (Britton and others 2010) and invasive plant pathogens (Klopfenstein and others 2010). Similarly, a summary of invasive species research and an expertise directory for the RMRS was recently published (Butler and others 2009), which included a section on invasive pathogen research (Klopfenstein and Geils 2009). RMRS has also contributed to regional forest pathology groups, such as Western International Forest Disease Work Conference, which cover diverse aspects of invasive pathogens (Geils 2004b). In another review paper, several authors from Federal and State institutions produced a collaborative review on impacts of non-native invasive species on U.S. forests (Moser and others 2009). This review addresses ecological, economic, and social impacts of invasive species such as pathogens, insects, plants, and aquatic organisms in forests. Recommendations for policy and management were provided.

RMRS research programs have developed critical information for four key areas of invasive pathogens and microbes.

(1) Prediction and Prevention. Because invasive pathogens are virtually impossible to eradicate after establishment, predicting and preventing them is the most efficacious method to minimize impacts. However, considerable baseline information on precise distributions of hosts and pathogens and interactions with the environment is needed to develop effective prediction tools. When compiling inventories of pathogenic fungi, it is important to include pathogens that cause only minor disease problems, because invasive pathogens frequently cause only minor damage in the area of their origin. Also, representative samples are needed for pathogens that are widespread, because subspecies groups may exist that have distinct ecological behavior. Surveys of existing fungi of forests and nurseries are difficult to conduct because numerous species exist, fungal taxonomy is constantly changing, and species are difficult to identify accurately. However, DNA-based diagnostics provide a reliable and cost-effective means to survey existing pathogens (or hosts) within a region (Hoff and others 2004b). Because of the diverse utility of DNA-based characterization, it is extremely short-sighted to preclude DNA-based approaches from any pathogen survey.

Prediction of invasive pathogens requires an understanding of (1) current geographic distributions of forest pathogens and hosts; (2) genetic relationships among pathogen species, subspecies, and populations; (3) potential for intraspecific or interspecific hybridization to create novel pathogens with unique biological behavior; (4) genetic relationships among host species, subspecies, and populations; (5) environmental factors (e.g., temperature, moisture, soil types) that are suitable for survival, growth, and reproduction of forest hosts and pathogens; (6) how changing climate will affect the suitable climate space for forest hosts and pathogens; and (7) pathways of pathogen movement and introduction.

Concepts to examine the genetic structure of hosts and pathogens at the landscape level have been developed (Klopfenstein and others 2001; Lundquist 2005b; Lundquist and Hamelin 2005a, 2005b; Lundquist and Klopfenstein 2001; Richardson and others 2005). DNA-based analyses are currently underway to examine the genetic relationship of white pine blister rust pathogens worldwide (Richardson others 2010b). Such studies will evaluate risks associated with new introductions and seek the evolutionary and/or geographic origin of white pine blister rust that was introduced to North America. Studies on the distribution of genetic groups of *Armillaria* spp., root-rot pathogens of diverse trees, are providing a framework to predict potentially invasive pathogens and hybrids (Hanna and others 2007b; Hanna and others 2009). Studies are ongoing to examine the distribution and genetic relationships among *Armillaria* spp. in the Northern Hemisphere (Cannon and others 2008).

Recently, considerable interest has developed on eucalypt rust (*Puccinia psidii*), also known as guava rust, ohia rust, or myrtle rust. Eucalypt rust has been introduced to Hawaii, where it poses a current threat to myrtaceous trees, which represent ~80% of the native forest in Hawaii. This pathogen is also the subject of worldwide concern, because of its capacity to infect eucalypts. Collaborative work with Universidade Federal de Viçosa (Viçosa, Brazil), Washington State University, the University of Hawaii, Forest Health Protection-Region 5, Western Wildland Environmental Threat Assessment Center, and RMRS is examining the population genetic structure of the eucalypt rust in Brazil, the putative origin of this rust, and other countries where the rust has been found. One goal of this project is to identify eucalypt rust populations that pose additional threat to Hawaiian forest and eucalypts (Cannon and others 2010; Graca and others 2010). Other evaluations were performed to assess the invasive risk of western gall rust (caused by *Peridermium harknessii*) to *Pinus radiata* in New Zealand (Ramsfield and others 2007). In addition, RMRS scientists were instrumental in developing a response plan for Scots pine blister rust, caused by a potentially invasive pathogen that is not yet present in the United States. (Geils and others 2009)

Other factors, such as climate and means of dispersal, must also be considered when predicting potentially invasive pathogens. Studies are underway that will use climate variables to predict areas with suitable climate space for invasive pathogens and evaluate potential effects of climate change (Klopfenstein and others 2009a). Other studies have investigated the possible mode of transport for invasive pathogens (Frank and others 2004, 2008; Geils 2004a).

(2) Early Detection and Rapid Response. Early detection of forest pathogens is dependent on identification to species, subspecies, and population level. Taxonomic identification of forest pathogens is largely dependent on herbaria and culture collections that allow comparisons among microbes. RMRS has a Forest Pathology Herbarium under the supervision of B.W. Geils. In addition, over 10,000 living culture archives of forest pathogens, endophytes, decomposers, and potential biological control agents are housed in the Forestry Sciences Laboratory in Moscow, Idaho. Because most forest pathogens and associated fungi cannot be easily detected or identified, techniques are needed to detect and identify forest pathogens and associated fungi (Kim and others 2005). DNA-based diagnostic methods were developed and/or applied for root rot fungi (Hanna and others 2007a; Kim and Klopfenstein 2011; Kim and others 2000, 2001, 2006, 2010a, 2010b, 2011; Klopfenstein and others 2009b; Stewart and others 2006), white pine blister rust (McDonald and others 2006; Zambino 2002; Zambino and others 2007a), powdery mildew pathogens (Mmbaga and others 2000, 2004), endophytes, and potential biological control agents (Hoff and others 2004a, 2004b; Stewart and others 2006).

RMRS research has contributed over 500 diagnostic DNA sequences to national databases to help in the identification of forest pathogens and microbes. These DNA-based diagnostic tools allow surveys of the present distributions of pathogens and microbes. These surveys are necessary to recognize an introduced pathogen and allow predictions of potentially invasive pathogens and microbes. Furthermore, such DNA-based diagnostic tools can be adapted for screening procedures designed to prevent movement of invasive pathogens and microbes.

One striking example of the need for DNA-based identification is associated with a conifer nursery (Stewart and others 2006). In this situation, isolates of *Fusarium commune* are highly pathogenic to Douglas-fir (*Pseudotsuga menziseii*), but morphologically indistinguishable from nonpathogenic *Fusarium oxysporum*. However, multiple DNA-based techniques were developed to detect and identify the pathogenic *Fusarium* species (Stewart and others 2006). Because nurseries represent a primary route by which invasive pathogens are spread, it is critical that DNA-based tools are used to survey pathogens that exist in nursery settings.

The utility of DNA-based diagnostics was also demonstrated with the white pine blister rust pathogen, *C. ribicola*. In North America, this pathogen was long assumed to utilize only *Ribes* spp. as its alternate (telial) host. Recently, natural infections of *C. ribicola* were found on three other alternate host species, *Pedicularis racemosa*, *Pedicularis bracteosa*, and *Castilleja miniata* (McDonald and others 2006; Zambino and others 2007a). The *C. ribicola* telia on these non-*Ribes* alternate hosts are morphologically indistinguishable from those produced by *C. coleosporioides*, an endemic pathogen that causes stalactiform rust on lodgepole pine (*Pinus contorta*) and utilizes *Pedicularis* spp. and *Castilleja* spp. as alternate hosts (Farr and others 1995; Vogler and Bruns 1998). Thus, DNA-based diagnostics were essential to recognize natural *C. ribicola* infection of non-*Ribes* alternate hosts in North America. Understanding the pathogen ecology and host utilization is essential to managing and predicting ecological behavior of invasive pathogens. RMRS scientists prepared a synthesis of molecular approaches for investigating white pine blister rust pathosystems (Richardson and others 2010a).

The fungal genus *Armillaria* is associated with diverse tree species worldwide. However, some *Armillaria* species are virulent pathogens, while others exhibit low pathogenicity and play beneficial roles in forest ecosystems. Thus, accurate identification of *Armillaria* species is a critical component of surveys of forest pathogens. Because many *Armillaria* species are difficult to identify by morphology, DNA-based techniques were developed to help identify *Armillaria* species (Kim and others 2000, 2001, 2006). These techniques were used to identify *Armillaria* species collected in a survey of *Armillaria* spp. in the inland northwestern United States. Surprisingly, an area in south-central Idaho was identified where the primary pathogenic *Armillaria* species (*A. solidipes* = *A. ostoyae*) was not found, even though suitable habitat types, suitable host trees, and other *Armillaria* species were present (McDonald and others 1987). Based on this information it appears that any introduction of *A. solidipes* into south-central Idaho represents an invasive species risk. This situation also emphasizes the key role of DNA-based diagnostic methods for pathogen surveys, without which this unique phenomenon would remain unrecognized.

(3) Control and Management. Because of the enormous and growing impacts of white pine blister rust, considerable research in RMRS has be devoted to control and management of this disease that impacts diverse forest ecosystems that comprise several species of five-needled white pines (Geils 2001, 2003; Hoff and others 2001; Kendall and Keane 2001; McCaughey and Schmidt 2001; Schoettle 2004a; Tomback and others 2001a; Zambino and McDonald 2003). Continuing studies have documented the spread of white pine blister rust (Geils 2000; Geils and others 2003; Kearns and Jacobi 2007) and the development of hazard rating systems (Van Arsdale and others 2006). Additional studies have been conducted on infection episodes of comandra rust, a related native rust disease, on lodgepole pine (Jacobi and others 2002). A white pine blister rust model has been developed that simulates the life cycle of the pathogen and resulting tree mortality (McDonald and others 1981), and further developments of this model are still in use as an extension to the Forest Vegetation Simulator (FVS; http://www.fs.fed.us/foresthealth/technology/wpbr_model.shtml). Research on disease resistance has contributed to breeding programs of western white pine and eastern white pine (Hudgins and others 2005; Jurgens and others 2003; McDonald and others 2004; Woo and others 2001, 2002, 2004a, 2004b), and genetic research has evaluated the impact of resistance breeding on the genetic diversity of western white pine (Kim and others 2003). Research by RMRS scientists to assess resistance in limber pine and Rocky Mountain bristlecone pine is ongoing (Sniezko and others 2008; Vogler and others 2006; Schoettle and others 2007; Schoettle and others 2009). Methods to identify genetic markers for rust resistance have been developed for other tree species (Tabor and others 2000). Because the white pine blister rust pathogen requires an alternate host to complete its lifecycle, research has documented the distribution and role of *Ribes* spp. in this disease (Van Arsdel and Geils 2004; Zambino 2010). Recently, other alternate hosts of white pine blister rust were confirmed in North America (McDonald and others 2006; Zambino and others 2007a). This finding may significantly impact our understanding of risks posed by this disease (Kearns and others 2004; Zambino and others 2006, 2007b). Genetic research is assessing whether the blister rust pathogen is changing in a manner that could affect disease development, potential risks of new introductions, and genetic relationships among pathogen populations (Hamelin and others 2000; McDonald 2000; Richardson 2006; Richardson and others 2007, 2008a).

Other research is being directed toward developing proactive approaches in management of high-elevation white pines to reduce the impact of white pine blister rust (Schoettle 2004b; Schoettle and Sniezko 2007; Schoettle and others 2007; Schoettle and others 2009). This new intervention paradigm moves past the idea of protecting the hosts from exposure to the established non-native invader and shifts toward facilitating naturalization by preparing the landscape to sustain ecosystem function into the future in the presence of the invasive. For white pine blister rust, this means facilitating evolution of genetic resistance in the pine host to the non-native pathogen. Positioning the ecosystem for greater resilience upon invasion is especially important for traditionally minimally managed ecosystems where the risk of ecological impacts is high. These ecosystems may be remote but they are not out of reach for invasion by non-native organisms.

Science information has been synthesized for various users and forest managers. A website established by B.W. Geils entitled "The Peridium" contains diverse information about rust diseases and their management (http://www.rms.nau.edu/rust/). A website developed by A.W. Schoettle is devoted to high-elevation white pines, their ecosystems, and the factors that threaten them (http://www fs.fed.us/rm/highelevationwhitepines/index htm). Information about whitebark pine was also compiled in book form (Tomback and others 2001b). In addition, B.W. Geils has established an RMRS database that contains comprehensive historical publications related to white pine blister rust. USDA research on biological control of native and invasive pathogens was also summarized (Klopfenstein and others 2000).

Other pathogens, such as *Armillaria* spp. and other root pathogens, have the potential to behave as invasive pathogens following disturbances, such as fire or fuels treatment. Science-based syntheses have developed reports and online tools to guide managers in the application of fuels treatments and potential impacts on root disease (*Armillaria* Response Tool http://forest.moscowfsl.wsu.edu/fuels/art/; Rippy and others 2005; McDonald and others 2005). A number of studies have developed methods and models to evaluate the effects of disease-induced disturbances at various landscape scales (Kallas and others 2003; Lundquist 2000, 2005a; Lundquist and Beatty 2002; Lundquist and Hamelin 2005a, 2005b; Lundquist and Lindner 2000; Lundquist and Negron 2000; Lundquist and Sommerfeld 2002; Reich and Lundquist 2005). Other studies have developed methods to assess non-timber impacts of disease (Lundquist and Ward 2005; Stubblefield and others 2005).

(4) Rehabilitation and Restoration. Information has been compiled for restoration of forest ecosystems impacted by white pine blister rust (Arno and others 2001; Burns and others 2008; Conklin and others 2009; Fins and others 2002; Harvey and others 2008; Keane 2001; Keane and Arno 2001; McCaughey and Tomback 2001; Neuenschwander and others 1999; Tomback and others 2001b; Wagner and others 2000). Science synthesis reports have been developed to demonstrate how molecular genetic tools can contribute to rehabilitation and restoration (Kim and others 2005; Richardson and others 2005). RMRS research has been active in defining host populations that are affected by white pine blister rust, such as white bark pine (Dekker-Robertson and Bruederle 2001; Richardson 2001; Richardson and others 2002a), western white pine (Kim and others 2003, 2011), and limber pine (Schoettle and Rochelle 2000). Understanding of population dynamics and capacity for regeneration is critical to sustaining healthy ecosystems and restoring impacted ecosystems (Coop and Schoettle 2009; Coop and others 2010; Richardson and others 2002b). Fire-scar and tree-recruitment chronologies have been developed from two limber and bristlecone pine sites in Colorado (Brown and Schoettle 2008). Population structures in both sites document relationships with disturbances and changes in climate and land use over the past several centuries, and they provide the longest such records yet developed for this area of North America. A population genetic model parameterized for the high elevation white pines is being constructed to examine the effects of white pine blister rust on the ecological and evolutionary dynamic of rust resistance in the pines (Antolin and others 2009; Schoettle and others 2010). Incorporation of these natural disturbance regimes with management intervention is critical to the long-term sustainability of the host population in the presence of the invasive species (Coop and Schoettle 2009). Lessons learned from long-term research toward enhancing natural recovery of impacted ecosystems has been synthesized for management professionals (McDonald and others 2005; McDonald and Hoff 2001; Zambino and McDonald 2003).

Genetic conservation is an important strategy for sustaining white pines threatened by white pine blister rust and other stressors. RMRS scientists and cooperators are developing and applying molecular and quantitative tools for investigating genetic diversity, correlations among adaptive traits, and disease resistance in several species of white pines. Kim and others (2011) examined the range-wide genetic diversity of western white pine (*Pinus monticola*) populations across the western United States. In related studies, Richardson and others (2009) demonstrated that spatial patterns of western white pine derived from molecular and quantitative genetic data were congruent with regional climates. Issues related to the conservation of limber pine have been addressed by Schoettle and others (2008).

Ongoing research is addressing how climate change will further threaten forest ecosystems that are at risk from white pine blister rust (Richardson and others 2008b; Warwell and others 2007, 2008). Influences of other disturbances such as mountain pine beetle epidemics and climate change on management of white pine blister rust impacts is also being explored (Schoettle and others 2008).

Literature Cited

Anagnostakis, S.L. 1987. Chestnut blight: The classical problem of an introduced pathogen. Mycologia 79:23-37.

Antolin, M.F.; Field, S.; Klutsch, J.; Schoettle, A.W.; Tavener, S.J. 2009. A stage-structured model for spread of pathogens into naive populations. Ecological Society of America 94th Annual Meeting Proceedings. August 2-7, 2009; Albuquerque, NM. Available: http://eco. confex.com/eco/2009/techprogram/P19372.HTM.

Arno, S.F.; Tomback, D.F.; Keane, R.E. 2001. Whitebark pine restoration: A model for wildland communities. Chapter 20. In: Tomback, D.F.; Arno, S.F.; Keane, R.E., eds. Whitebark Pine Communities—Ecology and Restoration. Washington, DC: Island Press: 416-420.

Brasier, C.M.; Buck, K.W. 2001. Rapid evolutionary changes in a globally invading fungal pathogen (Dutch elm disease). Biological Invasions 3:223-233.

Britton, K.O.; Buford, M.; Burnett, K.; [and others]. 2010. Invasive species overarching priorities to 2029. In: Dix, M.E.; Britton, K., eds. A dynamic invasive species research vision: Opportunities and priorities 2009-29. Gen. Tech. Rep. WO-79. Washington, DC: U.S. Department of Agriculture, Forest Service, Research and Development: 3-11.

Brown, P.M.; Schoettle, A.W. 2008. Fire and stand history in two limber pine (*Pinus flexilis*) and Rocky Mountain bristlecone pine (*Pinus aristata*) stands in Colorado. International Journal of Wildland Fire 17:339-347.

Burns, K.S.; Schoettle, A.W.; Jacobi, W.R.; Mahalovich, M.F. 2008. Options for the management of white pine blister rust in the Rocky Mountain Region. Gen. Tech. Rep. RMRS-GTR-206. Fort Collins, CO: U.S. Department of Agriculture, Forest Service, Rocky Mountain Research Station. 26 p.

Butler, J.; Pearson, D.; Kim, M.-S., tech. eds. 2009. Invasive species working group: Research summary and expertise directory. Fort Collins, CO: U.S. Department of Agriculture, Forest

Service, Rocky Mountain Research Station. 20 p. Available: http://www.treesearch.fs fed. us/pubs/34540.

Cannon, P.; Klopfenstein, N.B.; Kim, M.-S.; Hanna, J.W.; Medel, R.; Alvarado-Rosales, D. 2008. An *Armillaria* survey in Mexico: A basis for determining evolutionary relationships, assessing potentially invasive pathogens, evaluating future impacts of climate change, and developing international collaborations in forest pathology. In: McWilliams, M.G.; Palaciou, P.; Quinney, S.J.; Quinney, J.E., comps. Proceedings of the 55th Western International Forest Disease Work Conference; October 15-19, 2007; Sedona, AZ. Salem, OR: Oregon Department of Forestry: 29-39.

Cannon, P.G.; Alfenas, A.C.; Graca, R.N.; Kim, M.-S.; Peever, T.; Klopfenstein, N.B. 2010. Determining if there are lines of guava rust (*Puccinia psidii*) that could seriously impact ohia (*Metrosideros polymorpha*) in Hawaii. In: Adams, J., comp. Proceedings of the 57th Western International Forest Disease Work Conference. July 20-24, 2009; Durango, CO. Fort Collins, CO: Forest Health Technology Enterprise Team: 47-49.

Conklin, D.A.; Fairweather, M.L.; Ryerson, D.E.; Geils, B.W.; Vogler, D.R. 2009. White pines, blister rust, and management in the Southwest. R3-FH-09-01. U.S. Department of Agriculture, Forest Service, Southwest Region. 16 p.

Coop, J.D.; Massatti, R.T.; Schoettle, A.W. 2010. Subalpine vegetation pattern three decades after stand-replacing fire: Effects of landscape context and topography on plant community composition, tree regeneration, and diversity. Journal of Vegetation Science 21:472-487.

Coop, J.D.; Schoettle, A.W. 2009. Regeneration of Rocky Mountain bristlecone pine (*Pinus aristata*) and limber pine (*Pinus flexilis*) three decades after stand-replacing fires. Forest Ecology and Management 257:893-903.

Daughtrey, M.L.; Hibben, C.R.; Britton, K.O.; Windham, M.T.; Redlin, S.C. 1996. Dogwood anthracnose: Understanding a disease new to North America. Plant Disease 80:349-358.

Davidson, J.M.; Werres, S.; Garbelotto, M.; Hansen, E.M.; Rizzo, D.M. 2003. Sudden oak death and associated diseases caused by *Phytophthora ramorum*. Online. Plant Health Progress. doi:10/1094/PHP-2003-0707-01-DG.

Dekker-Robertson, D.; Bruederle, L.P. 2001. Management implications of genetic structure. Chapter 15. In: Tomback, D.F.; Arno, S.F.; Keane, R.E., eds. Whitebark Pine Communities—Ecology and Restoration. Washington, DC: Island Press: 310-324.

Dix, M.E.; Britton, K., eds. 2010. A dynamic invasive species research vision: Opportunities and priorities 2009-29. Gen. Tech. Rep. WO-79. Washington, DC: U.S. Department of Agriculture, Forest Service, Research and Development. 130 p.

Farr, D.F.; Bills, G.F.; Chamuris, G.P.; Rossman, A.Y. 1995. Fungi on Plants and Plant Products in the United States. St. Paul, MN: APS Press. 1252 p.

Fins, L.; Byler, J.; Ferguson, D.; Harvey, A.; Mahalovich, M.F.; McDonald, G.I.; Miller, D.; Schwandt, J.; Zack, A. 2002. Return of the giants: Restoring western white pine to the Inland Northwest. Journal of Forestry 100:20-26.

Frank, K.L.; Geils, B.W.; Kalkstein, L.S.; Thistle, H.W., Jr. 2008. Synoptic climatology of the long-distance dispersal of white pine blister rust II. Combination of surface and upper-level conditions. International Journal of Biometeorology 52:653-666.

Frank, K.L.; Kalkstein, L.S.; Geils, B.W.; Thistle, H.; Van Arsdel, E.P. 2004. Could white pine blister rust spread by atmospheric transport from California to New Mexico? In: Geils, B.W., comp. Proceedings of the 51st Western International Forest Disease Work Conference: August 18-22, 2003: Grants Pass, OR. Flagstaff, AZ: 63-65.

Furnier, G.R.; Stolz, A.M.; Mustaphi, R.M.; Ostry, M.E. 1999. Genetic evidence that butternut canker was recently introduced into North America. Canadian Journal of Botany 77:783-785.

Geils, B.W. 2000. Establishment of white pine blister rust in New Mexico. HortTechnology 10(3):528-529.

Geils, B.W. 2001. Impacts of white pine blister rust. In: Fosbroke, S.L.C.; Gottschalk, K.W., eds. Proceedings of the U.S. Department of Agriculture Interagency Research Forum on

Gypsy Moth and Other Invasive Species 2001. January 16-19, 2001; Annapolis, MD. Gen. Tech. Rep. NE-285. Newton Square, PA: U.S. Department of Agriculture, Forest Service, Northeastern Research Station: 61-64.

Geils, B.W. 2003. Pathology of white pine blister rust. In: Proceedings of Whitebark and Limber Pine Workshop. February 18-19, 2003; Calgary, Alberta. Parks Canada: 17-23.

Geils, B.W. 2004a. How blister rust spreads. Nutcracker Notes 6:7,12.

Geils, B.W., comp. 2004b. Proceedings of the 51st Western International Forest Disease Work Conference; August 18-22, 2003; Grants Pass, OR. Flagstaff, AZ. 184 p.

Geils, B.W.; Conklin, D.; Frank, K.; [and others]. 2003. New information on the distribution of white pine blister rust for 2002. In: Stone, J.; Maffei, H. comps. Proceedings of the 50th Western International Forest Disease Work Conference. October 7-11, 2002; Powell River. Bend, OR: 94-99.

Geils, B.W.; Hummer, K.E.; Hunt, R.S. 2010. White pines, *Ribes*, and blister rust: A review and synthesis. Forest Pathology 40:147-185.

Geils, B.A.; Klopfenstein, N.B.; Kim, M.-S.; Spaine, P.; Richardson, B.A.; Zambino, P.J.; Shaw, C.G.; Walla, J.; Bulluck, R.; Redmond, L.; Smith, K. 2009. Recovery plan for Scots pine blister rust caused by *Cronartium flaccidum* and *Peridermium pini*. National Plant Disease Recovery System, a cooperative project of The American Phytopathological Society and The United States Department of Agriculture. Available: http://www.ars.usda. gov/SP2UserFiles/Place/00000000/opmp/Scots%20Pine%20blister%20rust%2090312. pdf.

Gordon, T.R.; Storer, A.J.; Wood, D.L. 2001. The pitch canker epidemic in California. Plant Disease 85:1128-1139.

Graca, R.N.; Ross-Davis, A.L.; Kim, M.-S.; Alfenas, A.C.; Peever, T.L.; Cannon, P.G.; Klopfenstein, N.B. 2010. Molecular population genetics of guava rust (*Puccinia psidii*): An invasive pathogen of native Hawaiian forests and a potential threat to eucalypts world-wide. In: Moricca, S., comp. Program and abstracts of the IUFRO 4th International Rusts of Forest Trees Working Party Conference. May 3-6, 2010; Università degli Studi di Firenze, Florence, Italy: 31.

Hamelin, R.C.; Hunt, R.S.; Geils, B.W.; Jensen, G.D.; Jacobi, V.; Lecours, N. 2000. Barrier to gene flow between eastern and western populations of *Cronartium ribicola* in North America. Phytopathology 90:1073-1078.

Hamelin, R.C.; Lecours, N.; Laflamme, G. 1998. Molecular evidence of distinct introductions of the European race of *Gremmeniella abietina* into North America. Phytopathology 88:582-588.

Hanna, J.W.; Klopfenstein, N.B.; Kim, M.-S. 2007a. First report of the root-rot pathogen, *Armillaria nabsnona*, from Hawai'i. Plant Disease 91:634.

Hanna, J.W.; Klopfenstein, N.B.; Kim, M.-S.; McDonald, G.I.; Moore, J.A. 2007b. Phylogeographic patterns of *Armillaria ostoyae* in the western United States. Forest Pathology 37:192-216.

Hanna, J.W.; Smith, A.L.; Maffei, H.M.; M.S. Kim, M.-S.; Klopfenstein, N.B. 2009. Survey of *Armillaria* spp. in the Oregon East Cascades: Baseline data for predicting climatic influences on Armillaria root disease. In: Baker, F.; Jamieson, C.; Palacios, P., comps, Proceedings of the 56th Annual Western International Forest Disease Work Conference. October 27-31, 2008; Missoula, MT: 53-59.

Harvey, A.E.; Byler, J.W.; McDonald, G.I.; Neuenschwander, L.F.; Tonn, J.R. 2008. Death of an ecosystem: Perspectives on western white pine ecosystems of North America at the end of the Twentieth Century. Gen. Tech. Rep. RMRS-GTR-208. Fort Collins, CO: U.S. Department of Agriculture, Forest Service, Rocky Mountain Research Station. 10 p.

Hoff, R.J.; Ferguson, D.E.; McDonald, G.I.; Keane, R.E. 2001. Strategies for managing whitebark pine blister rust. In: Tomback, D.F.; Arno, S.F.; Keane, R.E., eds. Whitebark Pine Communities—Ecology and Restoration. Washington, DC: Island Press: 346-366.

Hoff, J.A.; Klopfenstein, N.B.; McDonald, G.I.; Tonn, J.R.; Kim, M.-S.; Zambino, P.J.; Hessburg, P.F.; Rogers, J.D.; Peever, T.L.; Carris, L.M. 2004a. Fungal endophytes in woody roots of Douglas-fir (*Pseudotsuga menziesii*) and ponderosa pine (*Pinus ponderosa*). Forest Pathology 34:255-271.

Hoff, J.A.; Klopfenstein, N.B.; Tonn, J.R.; McDonald, G.I.; Zambino, P.J.; Rogers, J.D.; Peever, T.L.; Carris, L.M. 2004b. Roles of woody root-associated fungi in forest ecosystem processes: Recent advances in fungal identification. Res. Pap. RMRS-RP-47. Fort Collins, CO: U.S. Department of Agriculture, Forest Service, Rocky Mountain Research Station. 6 p.

Hudgins, J.W.; McDonald, G.I.; Zambino, P.J.; Klopfenstein, N.B.; Franceschi, V.R. 2005. Anatomical and cellular responses of *Pinus monticola* stem tissues to invasion by *Cronartium ribicola* J.C. Fisch. Forest Pathology 35:423-443.

Hunt, R.S.; Geils, B.W.; Hummer, K.E. 2010. White pines, *Ribes*, and blister rust: Integration and action. Forest Pathology 40:402-417.

Jacobi, W.R.; Geils, B.W.; Taylor, J.E. 2002. Frequency of comandra blister rust infection episodes on lodgepole pine. Res. Pap. RMRS-RP-36. Fort Collins, CO: U.S. Department of Agriculture, Forest Service, Rocky Mountain Research Station. 13 p.

Jurgens, J.A.; Blanchette, R.A.; Zambino, P.J.; David, A. 2003. Histology of white pine blister rust in needles of resistant and susceptible eastern white pine. Plant Disease 87:1026-1030.

Kallas, M.A.; Reich, R.M.; Jacobi, W.R.; Lundquist, J.E. 2003. Modeling the probability of observing Armillaria root disease in the Black Hills. Forest Pathology 33:241-252.

Keane, R.E. 2001. Successional dynamics: Modeling and anthropogenic threat. Chapter 9. In: Tomback, D.F.; Arno, S.F.; Keane, R.E., eds. Whitebark Pine Communities—Ecology and Restoration. Washington, DC: Island Press: 159-192.

Keane, R.E.; Arno, S.F. 2001. Restoration concepts and techniques. Chapter 18. In: Tomback, D.F.; Arno, S.F.; Keane, R.E., eds. Whitebark Pine Communities—Ecology and Restoration. Washington, DC: Island Press: 367-401.

Kearns, H.S.J.; Jacobi, W.R. 2007. The distribution and incidence of white pine blister rust in central and southwestern Wyoming and northern Colorado. Canadian Journal of Forest Research 37:462-472.

Kearns, H.S.J.; Jacobi, W.R.; Sullivan, K.; Geils, B.W. 2004. Is the alternate host for white pine blister rust present in Colorado? In: Geils, B.W., comp. Proceedings of the 51st Western International Forest Disease Work Conference. August 18-22, 2003; Grants Pass, OR. Flagstaff, AZ: 71-72.

Kendall, K.C.; Keane, R.C. 2001 Whitebark pine decline: Infection, mortality, and population trends. Chapter 11. In: Tomback, D.F.; Arno, S.F.; Keane, R.E., eds. Whitebark Pine Communities—Ecology and Restoration. Washington, DC: Island Press: 221-242.

Kim, M.-S.; Brunsfeld, S.J.; McDonald, G.I.; Klopfenstein, N.B. 2003. Effect of white pine blister rust (*Cronartium ribicola*) and rust-resistance breeding on genetic variation in western white pine (*Pinus monticola*). Theoretical and Applied Genetics 106:1004-1010.

Kim, M.-S.; Klopfenstein, N.B. 2011. A. Molecular identification of *Armillaria gallica* from the Niobrara Valley Preserve in Nebraska. Journal of Phytopathology 159:69-71.

Kim, M.-S., Klopfenstein, N.B.; Hamelin, R.C. 2005. Application of molecular genetic tools to studies of forest pathosystems. Chapter 2. In: Lundquist, J.E.; Hamelin, R.C., eds. Forest Pathology—From Molecules to Landscapes. St. Paul, MN: American Phytopathological Society Press: 9-20.

Kim, M.-S.; Klopfenstein, N.B.; Hanna, J.W.; Cannon, P.; Medel, R.; López, A. 2010a. First report of Armillaria root disease caused by *Armillaria tabescens* on *Araucaria araucana* in Veracruz, Mexico. Plant Disease 94:274.

Kim, M.-S.; Klopfenstein, N.B.; Hanna, J.W.; McDonald, G.I. 2006. Characterization of North American *Armillaria* species: Genetic relationships determined by ribosomal DNA sequences and AFLP markers. Forest Pathology 36:145-164.

Kim, M.-S.; Klopfenstein, N.B.; McDonald, G.I. 2010b. Effects of forest management practices and environment on occurrence of *Armillaria* species. Journal Korean Forestry Society 99:251-257.

Kim, M.-S.; Klopfenstein, N.B.; McDonald, G.I.; Arumuganathan, K.; Vidaver, A.K. 2000. Characterization of North American *Armillaria* species by nuclear DNA content and RFLP analysis. Mycologia 92:874-883.

Kim, M.-S.; Klopfenstein, N.B.; McDonald, G.I.; Arumuganathan, K.; Vidaver, A.K. 2001. Use of flow cytometry, fluorescence microscopy, and PCR-based techniques to assess intraspecific and interspecific mating of *Armillaria* species. Mycological Research 105:164-172.

Kim, M.-S.; Klopfenstein, N.B.; Ota, Y.; Lee, S.K.; Woo, K.S.; Kaneko, S. 2010c. White pine blister rust in Korea, Japan and other Asian regions: Comparisons and implications for North America. Forest Pathology 40:382-401.

Kim, M.-S.; Richardson, B.A.; McDonald, G.I.; Klopfenstein, N.B. 2011. Genetic diversity and structure of western white pine (*Pinus monticola*) in North America: A baseline study for conservation, restoration, and addressing impacts of climate change. Tree Genetics and Genomics 7:11-21.

Klopfenstein, N.B.; Geils, B.W. 2009. Summary of taxa specific research 2. Pathogens. In: Butler, J.; Pearson, D.; Kim, M.-S., tech. eds. 2009. Invasive species working group: Research summary and expertise directory. Fort Collins, CO: U.S. Department of Agriculture, Forest Service, Rocky Mountain Research Station: 7-8. Available: http://www.treesearch.fs fed.us/pubs/34540.

Klopfenstein, N.B.; Juzwik, J.; Ostry, M.E.; [and others]. 2010. Invasive forest pathogens: Current and future roles of Forest Service Research and Development. In: Dix, M.E.; Britton, K., eds. A dynamic invasive species research vision: Opportunities and priorities 2009-29. Gen. Tech. Rep. WO-79. Washington, DC: U.S. Department of Agriculture, Forest Service, Research and Development: 23-33.

Klopfenstein, N.B.; Kim, M.-S.; Hanna, J.W.; Richardson, B.A.; Lundquist, J.W. 2009a. Approaches to predicting potential impacts of climate change on forest disease: An example with Armillaria root disease. Res. Pap. RMRS-RP-76. Fort Collins, CO: U.S. Department of Agriculture, Forest Service, Rocky Mountain Research Station. 10 p.

Klopfenstein, N.B.; Kuhlman, E.G.; Schumann, C.M.; Dix, M.E. 2000. III. Biological control of forest pathogens. A. Forest diseases. In: Coulson, J.R.; Vail, P.V.; Dix, M.E.; Nordlund, D.A.; Kauffman, W.C., eds. 110 Years of biological control research and development in the United States Department of Agriculture: 1883-1993. U.S. Department of Agriculture, Agricultural Research Service: 455-458.

Klopfenstein, N.B.; Lundquist, J.E.; Hanna, J.W.; Kim, M.-S.; McDonald, G.I. 2009b. First report of *Armillaria sinapina*, a cause of Armillaria root disease, associated with a variety of forest tree hosts on site with diverse climate in Alaska. Plant Disease 93:111.

Klopfenstein, N.B.; McDonald, G.I.; Kim, M.-S.; Brunsfeld, S.J.; Richardson, B.A.; Lundquist, J.E. 2001. Molecular genetic approaches to risk assessment in forest ecosystems. In: Proceedings of the Society of American Foresters National Convention. November 16-20, 2000. Washington, DC: 108-121.

Liebhold, A.M.; Macdonald, W.L.; Bergdahl, D.; Mastro, V.V. 1995. Invasion by exotic forest pests: A threats to forest ecosystems. Forest Science Monographs 10. 49 p.

Lundquist, J.E. 2000. A method of estimating direct and indirect effects of Armillaria root disease and other small-scale forest disturbances on canopy gap size. Forest Science 46:356-359.

Lundquist, J.E. 2005a. Patterns in diseased landscapes: A case study of a lodgepole pine forest infected by dwarf mistletoe: 145-153.

Lundquist, J.E. 2005b. Landscape pathology—Forest pathology in the era of landscape ecology. In: Lundquist, J.E.; Hamelin, R.C., eds. Forest Pathology—From Genes to Landscapes. St. Paul, MN: American Phytopathological Society Press: 155-165.

Lundquist, J.E.; Beatty, J.S. 2002. A method for characterizing and mimicking forest canopy gaps caused by different disturbances. Forest Science 48:582-594.

Lundquist, J.E.; Hamelin, R.C., eds. 2005a. Forest Pathology—From Genes to Landscapes. St. Paul, MN: The American Phytopathological Society. 175 p.

Lundquist, J.E.; Hamelin, R.C. 2005b. Forest pathology in the era of integration and synergy. In: Lundquist, J.E.; Hamelin, R.C., eds. Forest Pathology—From Genes to Landscapes. St. Paul, MN: American Phytopathological Society Press: 167-168.

Lundquist, J.E.; Klopfenstein, N.B. 2001. Integrating concepts of landscape ecology with the molecular biology of forest pathogens. Forest Ecology and Management 150:213-222.

Lundquist, J.E.; Lindner, L. 2000. Test of a model to assess the condition of lodgepole pine stands. Environmental Management 26:421-426.

Lundquist, J.E.; Negrón, J.F. 2000. Endemic forest disturbances and stand structure of ponderosa pine (*Pinus ponderosa*) in the Upper Pine Creek Research Natural Area. Natural Areas Journal 20:126-132.

Lundquist, J.E.; Sommerfeld, R.A. 2002. Use of fourier transforms to define landscape scales of analysis for disturbances: A case study of thinned and unthinned forest stands. Landscape Ecology 17:445-454.

Lundquist, J.E.; Ward, J.P., Jr. 2005. Impacts of diseases and other disturbances on non-timber forest resources: A case study involving small mammals. In: Lundquist, J.E.; Hamelin, R.C., eds. Forest Pathology—From Genes to Landscapes. St. Paul, MN: American Phytopathological Society Press: 105-112.

Maloy, O.C. 1997. White pine blister rust control in North America: A case history. Annual Review of Phytopathology 35:87-109.

McCaughey, W.M.; Schmidt, W.C. 2001. Taxonomy, distribution, and history. Chapter 2. In: Tomback, D.F.; Arno, S.F.; Keane, R.E., eds. Whitebark Pine Communities—Ecology and Restoration. Washington, DC: Island Press: 29-40.

McCaughney, W.M.; Tomback, D.F. 2001. The natural regeneration process. Chapter 6. In: Tomback, D.F.; Arno, S.F.; Keane, R.E., eds. Whitebark Pine Communities—Ecology and Restoration. Washington, DC: Island Press: 105-120.

McDonald, G.I. 2000. Geographic variation of white pine blister rust aeciospore infection efficiency and incubation period. HortTechnology 10:533-536.

McDonald, G.I.; Hoff, R.J. 2001. Blister rust: An introduced plague. In: Tomback, D.F.; Arno, S.F.; Keane, R.E., eds. Whitebark Pine Communities—Ecology and Restoration. Washington, DC: Island Press: 193-220.

McDonald, G.I.; Hoff, R.J.; Wykoff, W.R. 1981. Computer simulation of white pine blister rust epidemics. I. Model formulation. Res. Pap. INT-258. Ogden, UT: U.S. Department of Agriculture, Forest Service, Intermountain Forest and Range Experiment Station. 136 p.

McDonald, G.I.; Martin, N.E.; Harvey, A.E. 1987. Occurrence of *Armillaria* spp. in forests of the northern Rocky Mountains. Res. Pap. INT-381. Ogden, UT: U.S. Department of Agriculture, Forest Service, Intermountain Research Station. 7 p.

McDonald, G.I.; Richardson, B.A.; Zambino, P.J.; Klopfenstein, N.B.; Kim, M.-S. 2006. *Pedicularis* and *Castilleja* are natural hosts of *Cronartium ribicola* in North America: A first report. Forest Pathology 36:73-82.

McDonald, G.I.; Tanimoto, P.D.; Rice, T.M.; Hall, D.E.; Stewart, J.E.; Zambino, P.J.; Tonn, J.R.; Klopfenstein, N.B.; Kim, M.-S. 2005. Root disease analyzer—*Armillaria*. Res. Note. RMRS-RN-23-13WWW. Fort Collins, CO: U.S. Department of Agriculture, Forest Service, Rocky Mountain Research Station. 2 p.

McDonald, G.I.; Zambino, P.J.; Klopfenstein, N.B. 2005. Naturalization of host-dependent microbes after introduction into terrestrial ecosystems: Evolutionary epidemiology of white pine blister rust. Chapter 5. In: Lundquist, J.E.; Hamelin, R.C., eds. Forest Pathology— From Molecules to Landscapes. St. Paul, MN: American Phytopathological Society Press: 41-57.

McDonald, G.; Zambino, P.; Sniezko, R. 2004. Breeding rust-resistant five-needle pines in the western United States: Lessons from the past and a look to the future. In: Sniezko, R.A.; Samman, S.; Schlarbaum, S.E.; Kriebel, H.B., eds. Breeding and genetic resources of five-needled pines: Growth, adaptability, and pest resistance. Proc. RMRS-P-32. Fort Collins, CO: U.S. Department of Agriculture, Forest Service, Rocky Mountain Research Station. 259 p.

Mmbaga, M.T.; Klopfenstein, N.B.; Kim, M.-S. 2000. Molecular genetic analysis of powdery mildew pathogens of dogwood. In: Bryson, J.L., ed. and comp. Proceedings of the Southern Nursery Association Research Conference 45:236-242.

Mmbaga, M.T.; Klopfenstein, N.B.; Kim, M.-S.; Mmbaga, N.C. 2004. PCR-based identification of *Erysiphe pulchra* and *Phyllactinia guttata* from *Cornus florida* using ITS-specific primers. Forest Pathology 34:321-328.

Moser, K.W.; Barnard, E.L.; Billings, R.F.; Crocker, S.J.; Dix, M.E.; Gray, A.N.; Ice, G.G.; Kim, M.-S.; Reid, R.; Rodman, S.U.; McWilliams, W.H. 2009. Impacts of nonnative invasive species on U.S. forests and recommendations for policy and management. Journal of Forestry 107:320-327.

Neuenschwander, L.F.; Byler, J.W.; Harvey, A.E.; McDonald, G.I.; Ortiz, D.S.; Osborne, H.L.; Snyder, G.C.; Zack, A. 1999. White pine in the American West: A vanishing species— Can we save it? Gen. Tech. Rep. RMRS-GTR-35. Fort Collins, CO: U.S. Department of Agriculture, Forest Service, Rocky Mountain Research Station. 22 p.

Ramsfield, T.D.; Kriticos, D.J.; Vogler, D.R.; Geils, B.W. 2007. Western gall rust—A threat to *Pinus radiata* in New Zealand. New Zealand Journal of Forestry Science 37:143-152.

Reich, R.M.; Lundquist, J.E. 2005. Use of spatial statistics in assessing forest diseases. In: Lundquist, J.E.; Hamelin, R.C., eds. Forest Pathology—From Genes to Landscapes. St. Paul, MN: American Phytopathological Society Press: 127-143.

Richardson, B.A. 2001. Gene flow and genetic structure of whitebark pine (*Pinus albicaulis*): Inferences into bird-dispersed seed movement and biogeography. Thesis. University of Idaho, Moscow. 55 p.

Richardson, B.A. 2006. The white pine blister rust pathosystem: Assessing *Cronartium ribicola* genetic structure among different hosts and environments. Dissertation. Washington State University, Pullman.

Richardson, B.A.; Brunsfeld, S.J.; Klopfenstein, N.B. 2002a. DNA from bird-dispersed seed and wind disseminated pollen provides insights into postglacial colonization and population genetic structure of whitebark pine (*Pinus albicaulis*). Molecular Ecology 11:214-227.

Richardson, B.A.; Ekramoddoulah, A.K.M.; Liu, J.-J.; Kim, M.-S.; Klopfenstein, N.B. 2010a. Current and future molecular approaches to investigate the white pine blister rust pathosystem. Forest Pathology 40:314-331.

Richardson, B.A.; Kim, M.-S.; Klopfenstein, N.B.; Ota, Y.; Woo, K.S., Hamelin, R.C. 2010b. Tracking the footsteps of an invasive plant pathogen: Intercontinental phylogeographic structure of the white-pine-blister-rust fungus, *Cronartium ribicola*. In: Noshad, D.; Noh, E.W.; King, J.; Sniezko, R.A., eds. Breeding and genetic resources of five-needle pines. Proceedings IUFRO Working Party 2.02.15. September 22-26, 2008; Yangyang, Korea. Korea Forest Research Institute: 56-60.

Richardson, B.A.; Klopfenstein, N.B.; Brunsfeld, S.J. 2002b. Assessing Clark's nutcracker seed-caching flights using maternally inherited mitochondrial DNA of whitebark pine. Canadian Journal of Forest Research 32:1103-1107.

Richardson, B.A.; Klopfenstein, N.B.; Peever, T.L. 2005. Assessing forest-pathogen interactions at the population level. Chapter 3. In: Lundquist, J.E.; Hamelin, R.C., eds. Forest Pathology—From Molecules to Landscapes. St. Paul, MN: American Phytopathological Society Press: 21-30.

Richardson, B.A.; Klopfenstein, N.B.; Zambino, P.J.; McDonald, G.I.; Geils, B.W.; Carris, L.M. 2008a. The influence of host resistance on the genetic structure of the white pine blister rust fungus, *Cronartium ribicola*, in western North America. Phytopathology 98:413-420.

Richardson, B.A.; Rehfeldt, G.E.; Kim, M.-S. 2009. Congruent climate-related genecological responses from molecular markers and quantitative traits for western white pine (*Pinus monticola*). International Journal of Plant Science 170:1120-1131.

Richardson, B.A.; Warwell, M.V.; Kim, M.-S.; Klopfenstein, N.B.; McDonald, G.I. 2008b. Integration of population genetic structure and plant response to climate change: Sustaining genetic resources through evaluation of projected threats. In: Proceedings of Advances in Threat assessment and Their Application to Forest and Rangeland Management. July 18-20, 2006; Boulder, CO: 35-65.

Richardson, B.A.; Zambino, P.J.; Klopfenstein, N.B.; McDonald, G.I.; Carris, L.M. 2007. Assessing host specialization among aecial and telia hosts of the white pine blister rust fungus, *Cronartium ribicola*. Canadian Journal of Botany 85:299-306.

Rippy, R.C.; Stewart, J.E.; Zambino, P.J.; Tirocke, J.M.; Kim, M.-S.; Klopfenstein, N.B.; Thies, W.G. 2005. Root disease considerations for fuels treatments in western forests. Gen. Tech. Rep. RMRS-GTR-141. Fort Collins, CO: U.S. Department of Agriculture, Forest Service, Rocky Mountain Research Station. 32 p.

Schoettle, A.W. 2004a. Ecological roles of five-needle pines in Colorado: Potential consequences of their loss. In: Sniezko, R.A.; Samman, S.; Schlarbaum, S.E.; Kriebel, H.B., eds. Breeding and genetic resources of five-needle pines: Growth, adaptability, and pest resistance. Proc. RMRS-P-32. Fort Collins, CO: U.S. Department of Agriculture, Forest Service, Rocky Mountain Research Station: 124-135. Available: http://www.fs fed. us/rm/pubs/rmrs_p032/rmrs_p032_124_135.pdf.

Schoettle, A.W. 2004b. Developing proactive management options to sustain bristlecone and limber pine ecosystems in the presence of a non-native pathogen. In: Shepperd, W.D.; Eskew, L.G., comps. Silviculture in special places: Proceedings of the National Silviculture Workshop. September 8-11, 2003; Granby, CO. Proc. RMRS-P-34. Fort Collins, CO: U.S. Department of Agriculture, Forest Service, Rocky Mountain Research Station: 46-155. Available: http://www fs fed.us/rm/pubs/rmrs_p034/rmrs_p034_146_155.pdf.

Schoettle, A.W.; Antolin, M.F.; Klutsch J.; Field, S. 2010. A population genetic model for high-elevation white pines: Projecting ecological outcomes of restoration options. High-Five Symposium: The Future of High-Elevation Five-Needle White Pines in Western North America. June 28-30, 2010; Missoula, MT. Printed abstracts: 62.

Schoettle, A.W.; Burns, K.S.; Costello, S.; Witcosky, J.; Howell, B.; Connor, J. 2008. A race against beetles: Conservation of limber pine. Nutcracker Notes 14:11-12.

Schoettle, A.W.; Rochelle, S.G. 2000. Morphological variation of *Pinus flexilis* (Pinaceae), a bird-dispersed pine, across a range of elevations. American Journal of Botany 87:1797-1806.

Schoettle, A.W.; Sniezko, R.A. 2007. Proactive intervention to sustain high-elevation pine ecosystems threatened by white pine blister rust. Journal of Forest Research 12:327-336.

Schoettle, A.W.; Sniezko, R.A.; Burns, K.S. 2009. Sustaining *Pinus flexilis* ecosystems of the southern Rocky Mountains (USA) in the presence of *Cronartium ribicola* and *Dendroctonus ponderosae* in a changing climate. In: Noshad, D.; Noh, E.; King, J.; Sniezko, R.A., eds. Breeding and Genetic Resources of Five-Needle Pines Conference, IUFRO Working Party 2.02.15. September 22-26, 2008; Yangyang, Republic of Korea, Korea Forest Research Institute: 63-65.

Schoettle, A.W.; Sniezko, R.A.; Burns, K.S.; Freeman, F. 2007. Preparing the landscape for invasion–Early intervention approaches for threatened high elevation white pine ecosystems. In: Goheen, E.M.; Sniezko, R.A., tech. coords. Proceedings of the conference Whitebark Pine: a Pacific Coast Perspective. Aug. 27-31, 2006; Ashland, OR. R6-NR-FHP-2007-01. Portland, OR: U.S. Department of Agriculture, Forest Service, Pacific Northwest Region: 72-75. Available: http://www fs fed.us/r6/nr/fid/wbpine/proc.shtml.

Sniezko, R.A.; Kegley, A.; Danchok, R.; Schoettle, A.W.; Burns, K.S.; Conklin, D. 2008. *Cronartium ribicola* resistance in whitebark pine, southwestern white pine, limber pine and Rocky Mountain bristlecone pine—Preliminary screening results from first tests at

Dorena GRC. In: McWilliams, M.G., comp. Proceedings of the 55th Western International Forest Disease Work Conference; October 15-19, 2007; Sedona, AZ. Salem, OR: Oregon Department of Forestry: 84-86.

Stewart, J.E.; Kim, M.-S.; James, R.L.; Dumroese, R.K.; Klopfenstein, N.B. 2006. Molecular characterization of highly virulent isolates of *Fusarium oxysporum* from a conifer nursery. Phytopathology 96:1124-1133.

Stubblefield (Holte), C.H.; Lundquist, J.E.; van der Kamp, B. 2005. Forest disease impacts of wildlife: Beneficial? In: Lundquist, J.E.; Hamelin, R.C., eds. Forest Pathology—From Genes to Landscapes. St. Paul, MN: American Phytopathological Society Press: 95-103.

Tabor, G.M.; Kubisiak, T.; Klopfenstein, N.B.; Hall, R.B.; McNabb, H.S., Jr. 2000. Bulk segregant analysis identifies molecular markers linked to *Melampsora medusae* resistance in *Populus deltoides*. Phytopathology 90:1039-1042.

Tisserat, N.; Cranshaw, W.; Leatherman, D.; Utley, C.; Alexander, K. 2009. Black walnut mortality in Colorado caused by the walnut twig beetle and thousand cankers disease. Online. Plant Health Progress doi:10.1094/PHP-2009-0811-01-RS.

Tomback, D.F.; Arno, S.F.; Keane, R.E. 2001a. The compelling case for management intervention. Chapter 1. In: Tomback, D.F.; Arno, S.F.; Keane, R.E., eds. Whitebark Pine Communities—Ecology and Restoration. Washington, DC: Island Press: 3-25.

Tomback, D.F.; Arno, S.F.; Keane, R.E., eds. 2001b. Whitebark Pine Communities—Ecology and Restoration. Washington, DC: Island Press. 440 p.

Van Arsdel, E.P.; Geils, B.W. 2004. The Ribes of Colorado and New Mexico and their rust fungi. FHTET-04-13, Fort Collins, CO: U.S. Department of Agriculture, Forest Service, Forest Health Technology Enterprise Team. 32 p.

Van Arsdale, E.P.; Geils, B.W.; Zambino, P.J. 2006. Epidemiology for hazard rating of white pine blister rust. In: Guyon, J.C., comp. Proceedings of the 53rd Western International Forest Disease Work Conference. August 26-29, 2005; Jackson, WY: 49-64.

Vogler, D.R.; Bruns, T.D. 1998. Phylogenetic relationships among the pine stem rust fungi (*Cronartium* and *Peridermium* spp.). Mycologia 90:244-257.

Vogler, D.R.; Delfino-Mix, A.; Schoettle, A.W. 2006. White pine blister rust in high-elevation white pines: Screening for simply inherited, hypersensitive resistance. In: Guyon, J.C., comp. Proceedings of the 53rd Western International Forest Disease Work Conference. September 26-30, 2005; Jackson, WY. Ogden, UT: U.S. Department of Agriculture, Forest Service, Intermountain Region: 73-82.

Wagner, M.R.; Block, W.M.; Geils, B.W.; Wenger, K.F. 2000. Restoration ecology: A new forest management approach or another merit badge for foresters. Journal of Forestry 98:22-27.

Warwell, M.V.; Rehfeldt, G.E.; Crookston, N.L. 2007. Modeling contemporary climate profiles and predicting their response to global warming for whitebark pine (*Pinus albicaulis*). In: Goheen, E.M.; Sniezko, R.A., coords. Proceedings of the conference Whitebark Pine: A Pacific Coast Perspective. August 27-31, 2006: Ashland, OR. R6-NR-FHP-2007-01. Portland, OR: U.S. Department of Agriculture, Forest Service, Pacific Northwest Region: 139-142.

Warwell, M.V.; Rehfeldt, G.E.; Crookston, N.L. 2008. Modeling species' realized climatic niche space and predicting their response to global warming for several western forest species with small geographic distributions. In: Proceedings of Advances in Threat Assessment and Their Application to Forest and Rangeland Management. July 18-20, 2006; Boulder, CO: 36-59.

Woo, K.-S.; Fins, L.; McDonald, G.I. 2004a. Genetic and environmentally related variation in needle morphology of blister rust resistant and nonresistant *Pinus monticola*. In: Sniezko, R.A.; Samman, S.; Schlarbaum, S.E.; Kriebel, H.B., eds. Breeding and genetic resources of five-needled pines: Growth, adaptability, and pest resistance. Proc. RMRS-P-32. Fort Collins, CO: U.S. Department of Agriculture, Forest Service, Rocky Mountain Research Station: 148-153.

Woo, K.-S.; Fins, L.; McDonald, G.I.; Wenny, D.L.; Eramian, A. 2002. Effects or nursery environment on needle morphology of *Pinus monticola* Dougl. and implications for tree improvement programs. New Forests 24:113-129.

Woo, K.-S.; Fins, L.; McDonald, G.I.; Wiese, M.V. 2001. Differences in needle morphology between blister rust resistant and susceptible western white pine stocks. Canadian Journal of Forest Research 31:1880-1886.

Woo, K.-S.; McDonald, G.I.; Fins, L. 2004b. Influence of seedling physiology on expression of blister rust resistance in needles of western white pine. In: Sniezko, R.A.; Samman, S.; Schlarbaum, S.E.; Kriebel, H.B., eds. Breeding and genetic resources of five-needled pines: Growth, adaptability, and pest resistance. Proc. RMRS-P-32. Fort Collins, CO: U.S. Department of Agriculture, Forest Service, Rocky Mountain Research Station: 250-254.

Zambino, P.J. 2002. Dry grinding at near-ambient temperatures for extracting DNA from rust and other fungal spores. BioTechniques 33:48-51.

Zambino, P.J. 2010. Biology and pathology of *Ribes* and their implications for management of white pine blister rust. Forest Pathology 40:264-291.

Zambino, P.J.; McDonald, G.I. 2003. Resistance to white pine blister rust in North American five-needle pines and Ribes and its implications. In: Geils, B.W., comp. 2004. Proceedings of the 51st Western International Forest Disease Work Conference; August 18-22, 2003; Grants Pass, OR. Flagstaff, AZ: 111-125.

Zambino, P.J.; McDonald, G.I.; Richardson, B.A. 2007a. First report of the white pine blister rust fungus, *Cronartium ribicola*, on *Pedicularis bracteosa*. Plant Disease 91:467.

Zambino, P.J.; Richardson, B.A.; McDonald, G.I.; Klopfenstein, N.B.; Kim, M.-S. 2006. Non-*Ribes* alternate hosts of white pine blister rust: What this discovery means to whitebark pine. Nutcracker Notes Issue 10:6-7.

Zambino, P.J.; Richardson, B.A.; McDonald, G.I.; Klopfenstein, N.B.; Kim, M.-S. 2007b. A paradigm shift for white pine blister rusts: Non-*Ribes* alternate hosts for *Cronartium ribicola* in North America. In: Proceedings of the 53rd Western International Forest Disease Work Conference. September 22-30, 2005; Jackson, WY: 161-163.

III. INSECTS

By Jose F. Negrón

RMRS research on insect pests focuses mostly on conifer pests. There is a long history of invasive insects causing significant impacts, mortality, and changes in forest ecosystem structure in North America. Perhaps the most evident example is the introduction of the gypsy moth, *Lymantria dispar*, into eastern North America in the 1860s (Forbush and Frenald 1896). Although not well understood, it has caused shifts in forest structure and significant resources have been spent in management and control efforts that continue today (http://www.fs.fed.us/ne/morgantown/4557/gmoth/). The smaller European elm bark beetle, *Scolytus multistriatus*, was introduced into North America in the early 1900s (Chapman 1910). Coupled with Dutch elm disease, for which the insect is the primary vector (Readio 1935), it has caused the devastation of native elms across North America (Bloomfield 1979). The Asian longhorned beetle, *Anoplophora glabripennis*, and the emerald ash borer, *Agrilus planipennis*, are more recent introductions (Nowak and others 2001; Poland and McCullough 2006). The former has killed numerous maples, elms, and willows in New York and Chicago and the latter is destroying extensive areas of ash in Michigan and across the Midwest. The Sirex woodwasp, *Sirex noctilio*, which attacks several species of pines, was detected in 2004 (Hoebeke and others 2005) and is considered established in parts of Pennsylvania, New York, and Michigan (http://www.invasivespeciesinfo.gov/animals/sirexwasp.shtml). In the Rocky Mountain Region, the first detection of the banded elm bark beetle, *Scolytus schevyrewi*, occurred in 2003 (Negrón and others 2005). The insect utilizes various species of elms as hosts and tree mortality has been reported particularly in conjunction with drought. A number of other exotic bark beetles are established in North America (Wood 1982). Although none have been agents of extensive mortality, their ecological implications are not well known. Some other recent introductions to North America include the pine shoot beetle, *Tomicus piniperda*; the redhaired pine bark beetle, *Hylurgus ligniperda*; and the Mediterranean pine engraver, *Orthotomicus erosus* (Lee and others 2010). The mountain pine beetle, *Dendroctonus ponderosae*, a native disturbance agent in pine forests of western North America, is currently expanding its range into new areas of British Columbia and Alberta (Carroll and others 2004). Although there is evidence of historical mountain pine beetle outbreaks in high elevation five needle pine forests (Perkins and Roberts 2003), current trends in beetle-caused tree mortality appear unprecedented. Increasing temperature associated with climate change as it directly influences the insect is one important factor in mountain pine beetle range expansion and shifts in outbreak dynamics (Carroll and others 2004). Due to their extreme sensitivity to temperature, all forest insects will be directly affected by temperature increases. Moreover, climate change affects on forest insects may also manifest indirectly through affects to host trees. In addition to predicted changes in the geographic distribution of many tree species, climate change will also affect tree physiology and thus interactions with their herbivore predators (Mattson 1980; Zvereva and Kozlov 2006; McKenney and others 2007). Therefore, in a changing climate, many forest insects currently considered native may soon become invasive as their habitat changes.

Building a successful invasive species research program in entomology at the Rocky Mountain Research Station needs to be linked to the National Strategy and Implementation Plan for Invasive Species Management and must address the four national program elements:

(1) Prevention. There is some understanding of the major exotic species of concern that could impact our western forests. Pathway and risk assessments, such as the Exotic Forest Pest Information System for North America (http://spfnic.fs.fed.us/exfor/), have been initiated to identify priority insects. International commercial activities and unregulated transport of firewood are primary pathways for the movement of invasive insects; therefore, it is imperative to design educational programs that build public awareness of the problem. Climate change will affect host response, the likelihood of establishment of invasive insects, and the range expansion of native insects into new areas. The examination of how climate change may influence these processes is of utmost importance. At RMRS, studies are underway to examine how climate change will influence range expansion of mountain pine beetle and other bark beetles.

(2) Early Detection and Rapid Response. Between 1985 and 2000 there were almost 7,000 records of interception of exotic bark beetles by USDA APHIS (Haack 2001). These numbers will increase as worldwide commerce continues to expand. Tools in support of programs aimed at the early detection of insects such as the identification of pheromones or attractants for detection and monitoring will streamline and increase the efficiency of these programs. At RMRS, in cooperation with the PSW Research Station, we have been studying the chemical ecology of the banded elm bark beetle (Negrón and others 2005; Lee and others 2002). We continue to witness a precipitous decline in taxonomic expertise in wood-boring insects, and the available scientists are unable to address the demand for this service. This raises the need for developing taxonomic tools that can be used by personnel of agencies responsible for detection at ports of entry. In cooperation with APHIS, Colorado State University, and Forest Health, the RMRS has developed an image-based key to the Bark Beetle Genera of North America (Mercado 2010). Also in Cooperation with Colorado State University, at RMRS we are finalizing a "Revision of the Species in the Genus *Hylurgops* LeConte," which includes potentially important exotic species (Mercado, unpublished data).

(3) Control and Management. Available control strategies against established invasive insects are laborious, expensive, unsustainable, and of unknown efficacy. Streamlined approaches need to be developed to mitigate potential impacts, and just as importantly treatment success needs to be evaluated. As not every infestation can be targeted for control, decision support systems are needed to identify proper circumstances in which active management is warranted. Exploration of biological control approaches for managing invasive insects needs to continue. At RMRS, the work on range expansion of bark beetles will partly address the identification of new areas where management approaches may be needed. Scientists at RMRS also have the expertise to develop biological control programs targeted at potentially damaging exotic insects.

(4) Rehabilitation and Restoration. The identification of native host plant material resistant to invasive insects will be needed for use in re-vegetation programs of affected areas. In cases that this is not possible, identifying alternative plants and trees that could be used to restore affected ecosystems while minimizing ecological impacts will also be needed. Finally, we will need to develop long-term cultural control approaches for restoring affected areas. Implementation of these programs should be followed by an assessment of their efficacy.

Literature Cited

Bloomfield, H. 1979. Elms for always. American Forests 85:24-26, 48, 50.

Carroll, A.; Taylor, S.; Régnière, J.; Safranyik, L. 2004. Effects of climate change on range expansion by the mountain pine beetle in British Columbia. In: Shore, T.L.; Brooks, J.E.; Stone, J.E., eds. Mountain Pine Beetle Symposium: Challenges and Solutions. Victoria, British Columbia: Inf. Rep. BC-X-399. Victoria, British Columbia: Canadian Forest Service: 223-232.

Chapman, J.W. 1910. The introduction of a European scolytid (The smaller elm bark beetle, *Scolytus multistriatus* Marsh) into Massachusetts. Psyche 17:63-68.

Forbush, E.H.; Fernald, C.H. 1896. The Gypsy Moth. *Porthetria dispar* (Linn.). A report of the work of destroying the insect in the Commonwealth of Massachusetts, together with an account of its history and habits both in Massachusetts and Europe. Boston: Wright & Potter Printing Co.

Haack, R.A. 2001. Intercepted Scolytidae (Coleoptera) at U.S. ports of entry: 1985-2000. Integrated Pest Management Review 6:253-282.

Hoebeke, E.R.; Haugen, D.A.; Haack, R.A. 2005. *Sirex noctilio*: Discovery of a Palearctic siricid woodwasp in New York. Newsletter of the Michigan Entomological Society 50:24-25.

Lee, J.C.; Hamud, S.M.; Negrón, J.F.; Witcosky, J.J.; Seybold, S.J. 2010. Semiochemical-mediated flight strategies of two invasive elm bark beetles: A potential factor in competitive displacement. Environmental Entomology 39:642-652.

Mattson, W.J. 1980. Herbivory in relation to plant nitrogen content. Annual Review of Ecology and Systematics 11:119-161.

McDonald, G.; Zambino, P.; Sniezko, R. 2004. Breeding rust-resistant five-needle pines in the western United States: Lessons from the past and a look to the future. In: Sniezko, R.A.; Samman, S.; Schlarbaum, S.E.; Kriebel, H.B., eds. Breeding and genetic resources of five-needle pines: Growth, adaptability, and pest resistance. Proc. RMRS-P-32. Fort Collins, CO: U.S. Department of Agriculture, Forest Service, Rocky Mountain Research Station. 259 p.

McKenney, D.W.; Pedlar, J.H.; Lawrence, K.; Campbell, K.; Hutchinson, M.F. 2007. Potential impacts of climate change on the distribution of North American trees. BioScience 57:939-948.

Mercado, J.M. 2010. Bark beetle genera of North America. 2010. Online. Available: www.lucidcentral.org. [Accessed: July 20, 2010.]

Negrón, J.F.; Witcosky, J.J.; Cain, R.J.; LaBonte, J.R.; Duerr, D.A., II; Mcelwey, S.J.; Lee, J.C.; Seybold, S.J. 2005. The banded elm bark beetle: A new threat to elms in North America. American Entomologist 51:84-94.

Nowak, D.J.; Pasek, J.E.; Sequeira, R.A.; Crane, D.E.; Mastro, V.C. 2001. Potential effect of *Anoplophora glabripennis* (Coleoptera: Cerambycidae) on urban trees in the United States. Journal of Economic Entomology 94:116-122.

Perkins, D.L.; Roberts, D.W. 2003. Predictive models of whitebark pine mortality from mountain pine beetle. Forest Ecology Management 174:495-510.

Poland, T.M.; McCullough, D.G. 2006. Emerald ash borer: Invasion of the urban forest and the threat to North America's ash resource. Journal of Forestry 104:118-124.

Readio, P.A. 1935. The entomological phases of Dutch elm disease. Journal Economic Entomology 28:341-353.

Wood, S.L. 1982. The bark and ambrosia beetles of North and Central America (Coleoptera: Scolytidae), a taxonomic monograph. Great Basin Naturalist Memoirs, No. 6. 1359 p.

Zvereva, E.L.; Kozlov, M.V. 2006. Consequences of simultaneous elevation of carbon dioxide and temperature for plant-herbivore interactions: A metaanalysis. Global Change Biology 12:27-41.

IV. Aquatics

By Michael K. Young

The problem of invasive aquatic species has long been recognized by scientists at the Rocky Mountain Research Station. Fausch and others (2006, 2009) recently overviewed this issue. A point that often distinguishes nonnative aquatic species from nonnatives in other environments is that the presence of some species is frequently prized by managers and the public. For example, many sport fisheries in the Rocky Mountains are based on angling for nonnative brook trout, brown trout, or rainbow trout, which have been implicated in the loss of native cutthroat trout and bull trout (Dunham and others 2002; Rieman and others 2006). In some cases, "native" cutthroat trout are regularly introduced into previously fishless waters where they may displace other aquatic species, such as some native amphibians (Dunham and others 2004). The sometimes conflicting societal desires for protecting native species and providing recreational opportunities presents managers with many challenges, which are intensified by the increasing urbanization of the Rocky Mountains, growing demands for water, and altered precipitation and streamflow patterns driven by climate change. Thus, prioritizing where to conduct native species conservation—based on species habitat requirements, the ecological, evolutionary, and social value of particular populations, and habitat distribution and dynamics—represents a knowledge gap that needs to be addressed, for example with the group of decision models applied to systematic conservation planning (Peterson and others 2008).

Furthermore, much of the research on aquatic invasive species has focused on nonnative salmonid fishes. Little work has been done by RMRS on invasive algae. Given climate change forecasts for reduced late summer stream flows and warming temperatures, future waves of nonnative species invasions are likely to include coolwater and warmwater species of fishes that arrive via connected river networks or human-assisted transport e.g., smallmouth bass throughout the Pacific Northwest (Sharma and others 2009). Moreover, large numbers of other kinds of invasive aquatic organisms—crayfish, mussels, amphibians, macroinvertebrates, and nonindigenous pathogens—are already present or likely to appear. Little work in any of the four core areas has been done with respect to these taxa, although this may become a management and research priority in the near future.

(1) Prevention. The prevention and prediction of invasions of nonnative aquatic species are critical concerns of managers. Rocky Mountain Research Station scientists have contributed to providing information that addresses aspects of prevention and prediction. For example, because rivers and streams are linear networks, strategically placed barriers to fish movements can create upstream refuges for native fish. A critical issue is how the size and characteristics of the upstream network are related to long-term persistence of native fish populations (Peterson and others ongoing), which dictates where barriers to nonnative fish migrations should be placed. Yet perhaps as or more important to persistence of native fish populations is the retention of connectivity between different populations. This connectivity might permit demographic support for marginally productive populations from stronger ones or the re-founding of populations lost after environmental catastrophes. Hence, the management problem is not just where to build a barrier to fish movement, but whether to build one at all. To that end, researchers have constructed a decision model that quantifies the tradeoffs between the invasion of a nonnative species, brook trout, and the retention of migratory pathways for a native species, west slope cutthroat trout (Peterson and others 2008). Constructing similar models for other sets of native and nonnative species, and conducting the field research supporting this work, would assist managers in other parts of the Rocky Mountains.

Less work has been directed at predicting which nonnative aquatic species are likely to appear. This is in part because many nonnative sport fishes have already been widely distributed by management agencies and have access to many waters throughout the Rocky Mountains. Moreover, although stocking of nonnative species in waters containing native species has greatly declined, illegal transfers by anglers have increased in recent decades. Thus the suite of nonnative fishes likely to appear is well known, but whether they will successfully invade new or accessible waters is not. Recent and ongoing research (Rich and others 2003; Rieman and others 2006; Benjamin and others 2007; Wenger and others ongoing; Neville and others ongoing) is identifying how environmental characteristics (e.g., hydrologic regime, stream valley configuration, water temperature, land management, natural disturbance, and climate change) influence invasion success by brook trout. Similar work needs to be undertaken for other species.

__(2) Early Detection and Rapid Response.__ A focus of aquatic species research in RMRS has been quantifying detectability of fish species during sampling (Peterson and others 2004, 2005; Young and Schmetterling 2004; Rosenberger and Dunham 2005; Schmetterling and Young ongoing; Thurow and others ongoing). The objective of this work was to improve the reliability of electrofishing-based estimates of the presence or abundance of certain species of salmonid fishes, primarily federally threatened bull trout. Tailoring this work to address the presence or abundance of nonnative species such as brook trout, brown trout, or rainbow trout would be relatively straightforward but has yet to be done.

There remain two key problems with respect to early detection of nonnative fish species. First, using electrofishing-based sampling to establish presence tends to be labor-intensive and expensive, making it unlikely that large numbers of waters will be surveyed annually. Thus, early detection of invasions of nonnative fishes is unlikely unless particular sites are already being monitored for other purposes. Second, hybridization of native species with nonnative ones, such as bull trout with brook trout or westslope cutthroat trout with rainbow trout, is a great concern for managers. The loss of genetic integrity of populations of native species may be driven by the movements of hybridized individuals (Hitt and others 2003) that are often difficult to recognize during field sampling. Presently, genetic assessments of these fish are neither timely nor inexpensive enough to permit their use for monitoring the status of invasions of hybridized fish. Hence, a key management need is a cost-effective, broad-scale assessment of fish community composition and genetic status.

__(3) Control and Management.__ Research on the control and management of nonnative aquatic species was mentioned in conjunction with prevention, although relatively little work has directly addressed eradication or suppression of nonnative species. An exception has been the preliminary study on the effectiveness of pheromone-based removals of brook trout (Young and others 2003; Lamansky and others 2009). This research is modeled after insect control practices that rely on pheromone traps or lures. Refinement of this approach for brook trout and its extension to other species, as well as work on mechanical control of other nonnative fishes (Rinne and others ongoing) would fill a large void for managers, who at present have few tools for the effective control of nonnative fishes.

__(4) Rehabilitation and Restoration.__ Rehabilitating or restoring populations of native species following nonnative species removal has not been a focus of research or a widely expressed management need because populations have been reestablished following long-used fish stocking protocols. Nevertheless, research in this area may be required if restoring population characteristics such as genetic diversity or life history complexity become restoration targets. A potentially controversial problem that is largely unstudied involves habitat restoration, much of which is completed under the guise of improving habitat for fish species. Yet it is unknown whether such activities favor native or nonnative species. Similar work on the effects of natural disturbance, e.g., severe fire, debris torrents, and floods, indicated that native fishes responded more favorably following disturbance than did nonnative fishes (Sestrich and others in prep; Rinne and others in prep), suggesting that more stable, "restored" habitats may prove detrimental to native fishes when nonnative fishes are present (Dunham and others 2003; Rinne and others in prep). More comprehensive research on community responses to natural disturbance and human manipulation of freshwater habitats is necessary to satisfy information needs of managers.

Literature Cited

Dunham, J.B.; Adams, S.B.; Schroeter, R.E.; Novinger, D.C. 2002. Alien invasions in aquatic ecosystems: Toward an understanding of brook trout invasions and potential impacts on inland cutthroat trout in western North America. Reviews in Fish Biology and Fisheries 12:373-391.

Fausch, K.D.; Rieman, B.E.; Dunham, J.B.; Young, M.K.; Peterson, D.P. 2009. Invasion versus isolation: Trade-offs in managing native salmonids with barriers to upstream movement. Conservation Biology 23:859-870.

Lamansky, J.A., Jr.; Keeley, E.R.; Young, M.K.; Meyer, K.A. 2009. The use of hoop nets seeded with mature brook trout to capture conspecifics. North American Journal of Fisheries Management 29:10-17.

Peterson, D.P.; Rieman, B.E.; Dunham, J.B.; Fausch, K.D.; Young, M.K. 2008. Analysis of tradeoffs between threats of invasion by nonnative brook trout (*Salvelinus fontinalis*) and intentional isolation for native westslope cutthroat trout (*Oncorhynchus clarkii lewisi*). Canadian Journal of Fisheries and Aquatic Sciences 65:557-573.

Sharma, S.; Herborg, L.-M.; Therriault, T.W. 2009. Predicting introduction, establishment and potential impacts of smallmouth bass. Diversity and Distributions 15:831-840.

V. TERRESTRIAL VERTEBRATES

By Dean Pearson and Deborah Finch

Within the Interior West, terrestrial vertebrates do not represent a large number of invasive species relative to invasive weeds, aquatic vertebrates, and invertebrates. However, several invasive terrestrial vertebrate species do cause substantial economic and ecological damage in the U.S. and in this region (Pimental 2000, 2007; Bergman and others 2002; Finch and others 2010). About 28 species of mammals have been introduced into the U.S.; these include dogs (*Canis familiaris*), cats (*Felis catus*), horses (*Equus caballus*), burros (*E. asinus*), cattle (*Bos taurus*), sheep (*Ovis aries*), pigs (*Sus scrofa*), goats (*Capra hirus*), deer (*Cervus* spp.), rats and other small mammals (Drost and Fellers 1995; Layne 1997). In the Interior West, released burros and horses graze heavily on native vegetation, facilitating invasion by exotic annuals. Many invasive mammal species in the Interior West have escaped or were released into the wild; some have become pests by preying on native animals, by spreading diseases to native animals, by grazing on crops and native vegetation, by increasing soil erosion, or by damaging structures (Pimental 2007; Finch and others 2010).

Approximately 100 of the 1,000 bird species in the United States are exotic (Temple 1992; EPA 2005). Of the introduced bird species, only 5% are considered beneficial whereas the majority are considered pests. The most serious pest bird in the Interior West and throughout the United States is the exotic common pigeon (*Columba livia*), which inhabits most cities (Robbins 1995). Pigeons defecate on buildings, streets, sidewalks, statues, and cars; and they feed on grain. Pigeons act as reservoirs and vectors for human and livestock diseases, such as parrot fever, ornithosis, histoplasmosis, and encephalitis (Weber 1979; Long 1981). Another very recently introduced and expanding dove is the Eurasian Collared Dove (*Streptopelia decaocto*). This species has invaded North America at a record pace. In 1982, it arrived in Florida and has since rapidly spread to places as far as Montana and Alaska. The invasiveness of this species has raised concern over its potential impacts on native species, particularly related species such as the Mourning Dove, but currently very little is known about its impacts on natives. Some birds damage crops. Exotic European starlings (*Sturnus vulgaris*) are common throughout the Interior West where they cost millions in reduced grain production and displace native birds. Another exotic urban bird, the house sparrow (*Passer domesticus*) was introduced in 1853 to control the canker worm, but by 1900, it had become a pest. House sparrows damage plants in residential and public areas, consume wheat, corn, and fruit, and harass and displace native birds (Pimental 2000).

About 53 amphibians and reptile species have been introduced into the United States (Pimental 2000). Perhaps the most significant amphibian pest in the Interior West is the bullfrog (*Rana catesbeiana*). Originally native to eastern North America, the bullfrog has been introduced widely in the West. Bullfrogs are broadly generalist consumers implicated in the decline of native ranid frogs and the Mexican gartersnake (*Thamnophis eques*) (Rosen and Schwalbe 1995). Bullfrogs may expose native amphibians to increased levels of risk by spreading the chytrid fungus (*Batrachochytrium dendrobatidis*). Bullfrogs are suspected to be significant predators of hatchling and juvenile western pond turtles. Some invasive terrestrial animal species are exotic like European wild pigs, nutrias, rock doves, and European starlings, but many are native species like brown-headed cowbirds, common ravens, and red foxes that have expanded into new habitats. Anthropogenic factors contributing to native species becoming invasive include: direct human introductions into new regions (bull frogs, eastern fox squirrels), habitat alterations (coyotes, brown-headed cowbirds), food subsidies (common ravens), facilitation by introduced exotics (brown-headed cowbirds), artificial habitats such as telephone poles used for nesting (common ravens), and suppression of large predators that may facilitate range expansions (red foxes, raccoons). At present, there are relatively few studies within RMRS examining these issues as they relate to terrestrial vertebrate invaders.

(1) Prevention. Europe is the main source of North American exotic vertebrates. Recent studies suggest that new introductions of exotic mammals and birds from Europe to North America peaked in the mid 19th century and have since declined to very low levels (Jeschke and Strayer 2005). This suggests that most such introductions have already occurred or that contemporary laws are reasonably effective at preventing new exotic mammal and bird introductions. However, within the Rocky Mountain Region, certain exotic and native North American invaders are still expanding into new locations, e.g., Eurasian collared doves, European wild boars, bull frogs, common ravens, and brown-headed cowbirds. Research can contribute to addressing this problem by developing new understanding of the factors facilitating expansion of these invaders (Finch and others 2010). RMRS Scientist Deborah Finch led the recovery team for the southwestern willow flycatcher, a species often parasitized by cowbirds. The recovery plan included steps for preventing cowbird parasitism. Past RMRS research has documented the link between anthropogenic disturbance and brown-headed cowbird invasion (Tewksbury and others 1999). Current research is underway to determine the habitat and landscape factors influencing the presence and distribution of cowbirds, their hosts, host selection, and host reproductive success (Finch ongoing). However, current RMRS research examining the potential range expansion of other animal invaders is limited or absent.

(2) Early Detection and Rapid Response. Given the continued expansion of extant invaders, such as bull frogs and Eurasian Collared Doves, into new locations, development of methods to monitor for nascent foci of vertebrate invaders and rapidly address them is warranted. Past and current RMRS research has clarified the role of habitat in influencing where brown-headed cowbirds are present or absent and where hosts are not affected or are severely affected in southwestern river systems (Finch 1982, 1983; Finch and Stoleson 2000; Schweitzer and others 1998; Brodhead and others 2007). Other invasive species research in this area is lacking, however, but is justified based on increasing rates of new introductions of invasive species, including invasive vertebrates (Finch and others 2010). Climate change is likely to influence the movement or spread of some invasive vertebrates. Finch and others (2010) advocate research to detect migration of invasives into new areas as habitats shift in response to changing climates.

(3) Control and Management. Effective management of invasive vertebrates requires (1) understanding the biological and ecological factors that determine invader success so management can target those causal factors for control and (2) identifying the invader's impacts on native species to ensure that management actions effectively mitigate invader impacts. Past RMRS research has documented how variation in managed habitats impacts the distribution of brown-headed cowbirds and their hosts and influences which hosts are selected to be parasitized (Finch 1982, 1983; Finch and Stoleson 2000; Schweitzer and others 1996, 1998; Brodhead and others 2007). Such information is valuable in designing habitat management approaches that will limit cowbird brood parasitism. Current RMRS research is evaluating the impacts of brown-headed cowbirds on native birds to determine whether host species may need active intervention (Finch, ongoing). Other collaborative studies are evaluating factors that determine brown-headed cowbird success (e.g., Tewksbury and others 2006). Research is needed to determine mechanisms for invader success and quantify invader impacts for other species, such as bull frogs, that have increasing impacts in the Interior West. In addition, studies of invasive urban species are needed to determine the extent they will need to be managed in rapidly expanding urban environments such as Phoenix, Denver, and Las Vegas.

(4) Rehabilitation and Restoration. Rehabilitating and restoring native communities impacted by invasive terrestrial vertebrates requires understanding the invader's impacts and the capacities of native species to recover from these impacts once the invader has been effectively controlled or removed. RMRS research in this area is currently limited to studies evaluating whether cowbird abundance and impacts on hosts increase or decrease after restoration and whether restoration for other purposes (e.g., fuel reduction) has benefits in controlling cowbird parasitism (Finch ongoing). Additional research is needed for other invasive terrestrial animal species, especially in habitats where restoration is beneficial in controlling damage and also to determine whether restoration for other purposes has incidental effects, positive or negative, on invasive vertebrates.

Literature Cited

Bergman, D.; Chandler, M.; Locklear, A. 2002. The economic impact of invasive species to Wildlife Services' cooperators. In: Clark, L.; Hone, J.; Shivik, J.A.; Watkins, R.A.; VerCauteren, K.C.; Yoder, J.K., eds. Human conflicts with wildlife: economic considerations. Proceedings of the Third NWRC Special Symposium. National Wildlife Research Center, Fort Collins, CO.

Brodhead, Katherine M.; Stoleson, Scott H.; Finch, Deborah M. 2007. Southwestern willow flycatchers (*Empidonax traillii extimus*) in a grazed landscape: factors influencing brood parasitism. The Auk 124(4):1213-1228.

Drost, C.A.; Fellers, G.M. 1995. Non-native animals on public lands. In: LaRoe, E.T.; Farris, G.S.; Puckett, C.E.; Doran, P.D.; Mac, M.J., eds. Our living resources: A report to the nation on the distribution, abundance, and health of U.S. plants, animals and ecosystems. Washington, DC: U.S. Department of the Interior, National Biological Service.

Environmental Protection Agency [EPA]. 2005. Final list of bird species to which the Migratory Bird Treaty Act does not apply. Federal Register March 15, 2005. 70:49.

Finch, D.M. 1982. Rejection of cowbird eggs by crissal thrashers. Auk 99:719-724.

Finch, D.M. 1983. Brood parasitism of the Abert's towhee: Timing, frequency, and effects. Condor 85:355-359.

Finch, D.M.; Stoleson, S.H., eds. 2000. Status, ecology, and conservation of the southwestern willow flycatcher. Gen. Tech. Rep. RMRS-GTR-60. Ogden, UT: U.S. Department of Agriculture, Forest Service, Rocky Mountain Research Station. 131 p.

Finch, Deborah M.; Pearson, Dean; Wunderle, Joseph; Arendt, Wayne. 2010. Terrestrial animals as invaders and as species at risk from invasions. In: Dix, M.E.; Britton, K., eds. A dynamic invasive species research vision: Opportunities and priorities 2009-29. Gen. Tech. Rep. WO-79. Washington, DC: U.S. Department of Agriculture, Forest Service Research and Development: 43-54.

Jeschke, J.M.; Strayer, D.L. 2005. Invasion success of vertebrates in Europe and North America. Proceedings of the National Academy Science USA 102:7198-7202.

Layne, J.N. 1997. Non-indigenous mammals. In: Simberloff, D.; Schmitz, D.C.; Brown, T.C., eds. Strangers in Paradise. Washington, DC: Island Press: 157-186.

Long, J.L. 1981. Introduced birds of the world: The worldwide history, distribution, and influence of birds introduced to new environments. New York: Universe Books.

Ortega, Y.K.; Pearson, D.E.; Waller, L.P.; Sturdevant, N.J.; Maron, J.M. In press. Population-level compensation impedes biological control of an invasive forb and indirect release of a native grass. Ecology

Pimental, D.; Lach, L.; Zuniga, R.; Morrison, D. 2000. Environmental and economic costs of nonindigenous species in the United States. BioScience 53:53-65.

Pimental, David. 2007. Environmental and economic costs of vertebrate species invasions into the United States. Lincoln, NE: U.S. Department of Agriculture, National Wildlife Research Center Symposia, Managing Vertebrate Invasive Species. University of Nebraska.

Robbins, C.S. 1995. Non-native birds. In: LaRoe, E.T.; Farris, G.S.; Puckett, C.E.; Doran, P.D.; Mac, M.J., eds. Our living resources: A report to the nation on the distribution, abundance, and health of U.S. plants, animals and ecosystems. Washington, DC: U.S. Department of the Interior, National Biological Service: 437-440.

Rosen, P.C.; Schwalbe, C.R. 1995. Bullfrogs: Introduced predators in southwestern wetlands. In: LaRoe, E.T.; Farris, G.S.; Puckett, C.E.; Doran, P.D.; Mac, M.J., eds. Our living resources: A report to the nation on the distribution, abundance, and health of U.S. plants, animals, and ecosystems. Washington, DC: U.S. Department of the Interior, National Biological Service: 452-454.

Schweitzer, S.H.; Finch, D.M.; Leslie, D.M., Jr. 1998. The brown-headed cowbird and its riparian-dependent hosts in New Mexico. Gen. Tech. Rep. RMRS-GTR-1. Fort Collins, CO: U.S. Department of Agriculture, Forest Service, Rocky Mountain Research Station. 23 p.

Schweitzer, S.H.; Finch, D.M.; Leslie, David M., Jr. 1996. Reducing impacts of brood parasitism by brown-headed cowbirds on riparian-nesting migratory songbirds. In: Desired future conditions for Southwestern riparian ecosystems: Bringing interests and concerns together. September 18-22, 1995; Albuquerque, NM. Gen. Tech. Rep. RM-272: Fort Collins, CO: U.S. Department of Agriculture, Forest Service, Rocky Mountain Forest and Range Experiment Station: 267-276.

Temple, S.A. 1992. Exotic birds, a growing problem with no easy solution. The Auk 109:395-397.

Tewksbury, J.J.; Gardner, L.; Gardner, S.; Lloyd, J.D.; Saab, V.; Martin, T.E. 2006. Tests of landscape influence: Nest predation and brood parasitism in fragmented ecosystems. Ecology 87:759-768.

Tewksbury, J.J.; Martin, T.E.; Hejl, S.J.; Redman, T.S.; Wheeler, F.J. 1999. Cowbirds in a western valley: Effects of landscape structure, vegetation, and host density. Studies in Avian Biology 18:23-33.

Weber, W.J. 1979. Health hazards from pigeons, starlings and English sparrows: Diseases and parasites associated with pigeons, starlings, and English sparrows which affect domestic animals. Fresno, CA: Thomson Publications.

RMRS Invasive Species Research
Priorities and Future Directions

Presently, RMRS invasives research is conducted independent of other FS research stations because it focuses on issues and to some extent species largely unique to the region. Currently, 13.4 scientists (or scientist years) from six of the seven RMRS Programs (Air, Water, and Aquatic Environment; Fire, Fuel, and Smoke; Forest and Woodland Ecosystems; Grassland, Shrubland, and Desert Ecosystems; Human Dimensions; and Wildlife and Terrestrial Ecosystems) are conducting research on invasive species (Butler and others 2009). Since there is no RMRS program explicitly assigned to address invasive species issues, invasive species research in the Station has historically been ad-hoc with little coordination or communication across the Station regarding invasives research and with individual scientists struggling to obtain research support. To address this problem, and as a synergistic outcome of the Albuquerque Workshop that resulted in the current document, a group of scientists dedicated to invasive species research organized into the RMRS Invasive Species Working Group (ISWG). The ISWG is a cross-program multidisciplinary team formed to better integrate invasive species research across the Station with an emphasis on communicating research products to our customers. To date, the ISWG has developed two synthesis papers to summarize current RMRS research activities on invasive species: Butler and others (2009) and the current document. It has also established a website (http://www rmrs nau.edu/invasive_species) to disseminate research information and foster technology transfer, and it publishes a periodic newsletter (current and previous issues are located on the website) to familiarize and update customers with RMRS activities on invasive species and provide customers with contact information for feedback. It is hoped this collaborative effort will allow the Station to improve invasives management consistent with recommendations from the previous National Invasive Species Strategic Program Area Review. The establishment of this working group also provides a potential mechanism for building collaborations with other state and national invasive species efforts.

The organization of the RMRS ISWG has proven extremely valuable to date. It has not only greatly improved outreach efforts by the Station—it also holds the potential to facilitate more coordinated efforts on invasive species research and improve future research. For instance, the external review of the FS R&D invasive species research strategy (the National Invasive Species Strategic Program Area Review) recommended that FS expand its proactive research role (Prediction & Prevention, Detection & Rapid Response), while clearly maintaining its reactive research role (Management & Mitigation, Restoration & Rehabilitation). In response, the FS R&D research strategy emphasizes the following four overarching research priorities: (1) Quantifying invasive species biology, ecology, interaction, and impacts; (2) Predicting and prioritizing invasive species; (3) Identifying and detecting invasive species; and (4) Managing invasive species and altered systems. The RMRS invasives research has recognized strengths in overarching research priorities (1) and (4) and RMRS has recently produced significant advances in research priority areas (2) and (3). Proactive research is critical because it is much more economically efficient and logistically feasible. For this reason, these research areas warrant further expansion, and significant efforts are needed for education, training, and outreach. The ISWG recognizes these priorities as appropriate future directions and is committed to advancing invasive research and outreach to meet these objectives.

Literature Cited

Butler, J.; Pearson, D.; Kim, M.-S., tech. eds. 2009. Invasive species working group: Research summary and expertise directory. Fort Collins, CO: U.S. Department of Agriculture, Forest Service, Rocky Mountain Research Station. 20 p. Available: http://www.treesearch.fs fed. us/pubs/34540.